Biography Today

Profiles
of People
of Interest
to Young
Readers

Volume 15
Issue 2
April 2006

Cherie D. Abbey
Managing Editor

Kevin Hillstrom
Editor

Omnigraphics

615 Griswold Street
Detroit, Michigan 4822(

D1205784

Omnigraphics, Inc.

Cherie D. Abbey, *Managing Editor*
Kevin Hillstrom, *Editor*

Peggy Daniels, Sheila Fitzgerald, Laurie Hillstrom, Anne J. Johnson,
Sara Pendergast, Tom Pendergast, and Rhoda Wilburn, *Sketch Writers*
Allison A. Beckett, Mary Butler, and Linda Strand, *Research Staff*

* * *

Peter E. Ruffner, *Publisher*
Frederick G. Ruffner, Jr., *Chairman*
Matthew P. Barbour, *Senior Vice President*
Kay Gill, *Vice President—Directories*

* * *

Elizabeth Barbour, *Research and Permissions Coordinator*
David P. Bianco, *Marketing Director*
Leif A. Gruenberg, *Development Manager*
Kevin Hayes, *Operations Manager*
Barry Puckett, *Librarian*
Cherry Stockdale, *Permissions Assistant*

Shirley Amore, Kevin Glover, Martha Johns,
Kirk Kauffman, and Angelesia Thorington, *Administrative Staff*

Copyright © 2006 Omnigraphics, Inc.
ISSN 1058-2347 • ISBN 0-7808-0813-4

The information in this publication was compiled from the sources cited and from other sources considered reliable. While every possible effort has been made to ensure reliability, the publisher will not assume liability for damages caused by inaccuracies in the data, and makes no warranty, express or implied, on the accuracy of the information contained herein.

This book is printed on acid-free paper meeting the ANSI Z39.48 Standard. The infinity symbol that appears above indicates that the paper in this book meets that standard.

Printed in the United States

INDEXED IN
Children's Magazine Guide

Contents

Preface

Biography Today is a magazine designed and written for the young reader—ages 9 and above—and covers individuals that librarians and teachers tell us that young people want to know about most: entertainers, athletes, writers, illustrators, cartoonists, and political leaders.

The Plan of the Work

The publication was especially created to appeal to young readers in a format they can enjoy reading and readily understand. Each issue contains approximately 10 sketches arranged alphabetically. Each entry provides at least one picture of the individual profiled, and bold-faced rubrics lead the reader to information on birth, youth, early memories, education, first jobs, marriage and family, career highlights, memorable experiences, hobbies, and honors and awards. Each of the entries ends with a list of easily accessible sources designed to lead the student to further reading on the individual and a current address. Retrospective entries are also included, written to provide a perspective on the individual's entire career.

Biographies are prepared by Omnigraphics editors after extensive research, utilizing the most current materials available. Those sources that are generally available to students appear in the list of further reading at the end of the sketch.

Indexes

Cumulative indexes are an important component of *Biography Today*. Each issue of the *Biography Today* General Series includes a Cumulative Names Index, which comprises all individuals profiled in *Biography Today* since the series began in 1992. In addition, we compile three other indexes: the Cumulative General Index, Places of Birth Index, and Birthday Index. See our web site, www.biographytoday.com, for these three indexes, along with the Names Index. All *Biography Today* indexes are cumulative, including all individuals profiled in both the General Series and the Subject Series.

Our Advisors

This series was reviewed by an Advisory Board comprised of librarians, children's literature specialists, and reading instructors to ensure that the concept of this publication—to provide a readable and accessible biographical magazine for young readers—was on target. They evaluated the title as it developed, and their suggestions have proved invaluable. Any errors, however, are ours alone. We'd like to list the Advisory Board members, and to thank them for their efforts.

Our Advisory Board stressed to us that we should not shy away from controversial or unconventional people in our profiles, and we have tried to follow their advice. The Advisory Board also mentioned that the sketches might be useful in reluctant reader and adult literacy programs, and we would value any comments librarians might have about the suitability of our magazine for those purposes.

Your Comments Are Welcome

Our goal is to be accurate and up-to-date, to give young readers information they can learn from and enjoy. Now we want to know what you think. Take a look at this issue of *Biography Today*, on approval. Write or call me with your comments. We want to provide an excellent source of biographical information for young people. Let us know how you think we're doing.

Cherie Abbey
Managing Editor, *Biography Today*
Omnigraphics, Inc.
615 Griswold Street
Detroit, MI 48226

editor@biographytoday.com
www.biographytoday.com

Congratulations!

Congratulations to the following individuals and libraries, who are receiving a free copy of *Biography Today*, Vol. 15, No. 2, for suggesting people who appear in this issue:

Kay Altland, West York Middle School Library, York, PA

Mike Lajoie, Mansfield, MA

Nicole Nava, Austin, TX

BLACK EYED PEAS

William Adams (will.i.am) 1975-
Alan Pineda Lindo (apl.de.ap) 1974-
Jamie Gomez (Taboo) 1975-
Stacy Ferguson (Fergie) 1975-
American Hip-Hop Group
Creators of the Hit Records *Elephunk* and
Monkey Business

EARLY YEARS

The funky hip-hop group the Black Eyed Peas includes four
members: will.i.am (William Adams), apl.de.ap (Alan Pineda
Lindo), Taboo (Jamie Gomez), and Fergie (Stacy Ferguson).

While each of the Black Eyed Peas comes from a different cultural background, they all had similar experiences growing up. Each was raised by a single parent and grew up in a poor, working-class area in which they were in the minority. For each, their ethnic origins became an important part of their lives. These shared experiences made them more alike than different, which helped them form a strong bond as a group.

─────── " ───────

"The black people hung out by the lunch tables, the Mexicans hung out by the bathrooms, the white people hung out by their cars, the Asian people stood next to their lockers," will recalled about high school. "I would always wander between the different sections. If I didn't go to that school, Black Eyed Peas wouldn't be what it is."

─────── " ───────

will.i.am

will.i.am was born William Adams on March 15, 1975. His mother raised six children by herself, two of whom were adopted. will is African-American and grew up in a Mexican neighborhood in east Los Angeles. His mother set strict rules for will. She wouldn't allow him to wear any clothing with sports logos on it, and he wasn't allowed to wear sneakers either. She made him wear suits most of the time, especially for church every week. He has said that her strictness is the reason that he stayed out of trouble when he was growing up. He attended a mixed-race high school that was a 45-minute bus ride from his home. It was tough at the time, but today he credits his experiences there with helping him define his approach to music. "The black people hung out by the lunch tables, the Mexicans hung out by the bathrooms, the white people hung out by their cars, the Asian people stood next to their lockers," he recalled. "I would always wander between the different sections. If I didn't go to that school, Black Eyed Peas wouldn't be what it is."

apl.de.ap

apl.de.ap (pronounced "apple") was born Alan Pineda Lindo on November 28, 1974, in Sapang Bato, a small town north of Manila in Pampanga, Philippines. His mother, Christina Pineda, is Filipino, and his father was an African-American U.S. Air Force serviceman. His father left the Philippines before he was born, and apl never knew him. He lived with his mother and four brothers and two sisters in the Philippines, and the family struggled financially. apl was adopted by Joe Ben Hudgens, an American attorney who met apl's family through an organization that supports poor children in the Philippines. When he was a teenager, apl moved to Los Angeles, California, to live with his adoptive father. "I left in the afternoon," he recalled about the move, "and it was the saddest sunset ever. I didn't know where I was going. I was 14, and I'm getting on a plane by myself, and I could see the sun set." He struggled as a teenage immigrant. "I would get chased from junior high school to my house every day," he said. "You know, I could have easily joined the gangs that were surrounding me. I was exposed to that. But I chose dancing instead. That led me in a good direction."

Taboo

Taboo was born Jamie Gomez on July 14, 1975. He is Mexican-American and was raised by a single mother. Growing up in Rosemead, California, Taboo was taunted by the neighborhood kids, who made fun of him for being Latino but "dancing black." He didn't care too much what the other kids thought of him, and he continued to develop his break dancing talent. "I grew up in a predominantly Asian and Mexican community," Taboo recalled, "and because I did break dance and pop-lock and all that, I did get a lot of criticism: 'You're Mexican, why are you doing that?' I would say, 'It don't matter if you're Mexican, white, or black, I just like to dance.' It made me a stronger person. 'Oh yeah? Check this out.' It didn't matter, because I had that skill."

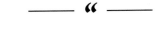

"*I would get chased from junior high school to my house every day," said apl.de.ap. "You know, I could have easily joined the gangs that were surrounding me. I was exposed to that. But I chose dancing instead. That led me in a good direction."*

Fergie

Fergie was born Stacy Ferguson on March 27, 1975. She is part white and part Native American. She grew up in Hacienda Heights, California, in a mostly Mexican and Asian neighborhood. Her parents, who were both teachers, separated when she was very young, and afterwards she and her mother had very little money. Growing up, Fergie wore mostly hand-me-down clothes that were given to her family by a local church. She began working in entertainment when she was eight years old, doing voice-overs for commercials and "Peanuts" television specials. She was a cast member on the Disney Channel's Saturday-morning television show "Kids Incorporated" for five years. After that, Fergie was part of Wild Orchid, an all-girl trio that produced two moderately successful albums in the late 1990s. Wild Orchid's pop music style included a lot of harmonizing, which led to comparisons with En Vogue, another female singing group that became popular in the 1990s. Despite the modest success of Wild Orchid, Fergie grew dissatisfied with the group and eventually quit. As a teenager, Fergie said, "I had my white girlfriends and my Mexican friends. . . . I'd go to the beach and to rock concerts, like Metallica, with my white girlfriends. Then I'd go dancing and to house parties with my Mexican girlfriends, and we'd listen to hip-hop and Lisa Lisa and Cult Jam and all that kind of stuff."

FORMING THE BAND

The group that eventually became the Black Eyed Peas was first formed when the boys were just teenagers. will and apl were both living in California when they met in the eighth grade in 1989. They shared the same intense interest in the emerging hip-hop scene and quickly became close friends. They joined a break dancing group called Tribal Nation and began performing around Los Angeles. They also spent a lot of time hanging out at the mall, practicing their dance moves. In fact, the two were routinely kicked out of the Glendale Galleria for break dancing.

———— " ————

As a teenager, Fergie said, "I had my white girlfriends and my Mexican friends.... I'd go to the beach and to rock concerts, like Metallica, with my white girlfriends. Then I'd go dancing and to house parties with my Mexican girlfriends, and we'd listen to hip-hop and Lisa Lisa and Cult Jam and all that kind of stuff."

———— " ————

"We were the only black family in a bad Mexican neighborhood," will recalled, "and apl was the only person my mum allowed me to hang out with because he was a foreigner. I went to good schools. apl was a good influence on my life. I wouldn't be here if he hadn't been sent to America; I would have had nobody to dream with. We would lie awake at night imagining the first time we'd go on stage in New York, and who we would thank if we got an MTV award."

After they graduated from high school, will and apl left the dance group Tribal Nation and created their own group, Atban Klann, which combined break dancing and rap. Atban was an acronym for A Tribe Beyond A Nation, their way of acknowledging their beginnings with Tribal Nation. By 1992, rapper Eazy-E signed Atban Klann to a contract with Ruthless Records. Atban Klann recorded an album, but it was never released. The album didn't fit in with the other Ruthless Records releases, or in any other music category either. Atban Klann's album featured dance tracks and positive raps while all of the other Ruthless artists were doing gangster rap, and the label simply didn't know what to do with will and apl. Eazy-E had been their only supporter at the label, but he was unable to get their record out. After Eazy-E died on March 26, 1995, Atban Klann ended their contract with Ruthless.

While searching for a new direction, will and apl met Taboo at a Los Angeles break dancing club. Taboo was a talented dancer and rapper who had been working odd jobs, most notably cleaning up horse manure at Disneyland and serving lunches in a high school cafeteria. will, apl, and Taboo soon became friends, and the three formed the Black Eyed Peas. The group reportedly had to come up with a new name because the name Atban Klann was owned by Ruthless Records as a term of their old contract. They chose the name Black Eyed Peas because it seemed to represent a humble connection to the soul community. (Black-eyed peas are a simple, popular soul food dish.)

CAREER HIGHLIGHTS

The Black Eyed Peas signed their first record contract with Interscope in 1997. Although their style had caused problems at Ruthless Records, the Peas were hopeful that their new record label would be more supportive. The trio of will, apl, and Taboo forged a new sound together, blending different musical styles and adding creative raps with positive themes. At that time, most other rap and hip-hop acts were focused on violent imagery and darker messages of urban ghetto life. The Peas were reaching back to the earliest days of hip-hop, when party music and dance tracks were the norm. They wanted to bring back some of those themes. "We like to have a good time, but we are positive, conscious people," will said. "Since rapping is what we do, people call us conscious rappers, and that's cool. That's who I am, a conscious person. If I were a plumber, I'd be a conscious plumber."

Early Releases

The Peas released their first record, *Behind the Front*, in 1998. The group had recorded about 50 songs between July 1997 and January 1998. They chose 16 tracks for the record, which music critics described as "food for the hip-hop soul." *Behind the Front* created a splash because it used live musicians at a time when most other hip-hop performers were using recorded backup sounds. The "relentlessly positive" raps also distinguished the Peas from other hip-hop groups. Their unique style could not be easily categorized. But instead of being a problem for them as it once was, it now allowed them to reach out and connect with many different audiences.

The Peas toured extensively to promote their new record. They were included in a few different multi-band traveling shows, such as the Smokin' Grooves hip-hop tour, the Sno-Core snowboard tour, the Lyricist Lounge hip-hop tour, and the Vans Warped tour featuring punk pop bands. The Peas also

The Black Eyed Peas in performance on the Warped Tour in 1999.

opened for OutKast on their tour. (For more information on OutKast, see *Biography Today*, Sep. 2004.) These live performances gave the Peas an opportunity to introduce themselves, and they quickly developed a national fan base. The tours also helped the Peas earn praise from the music industry. *Vibe* credited the Peas with "pushing the culture forward by incorporating funky-fresh dance steps and break dancing moves into their routines." And *Rolling Stone* said that "*Behind the Front* offers an organic mixture of sampled melodies and live instruments aimed at those of us seeking a little enlightenment with our well-oiled boogie."

The Peas released their second album, *Bridging the Gap*, in 2000. Will described the title as a reflection of American culture becoming more and more unified. "The suburbs are becoming urbanized, and urban doesn't mean black anymore, it means Latino, it means poor white folks, it means some Asian people. . . . The music is a bridge," will said. The title *Bridging the Gap* "means we're bridging the gap between rock and hip-hop." The record continued the Peas' tradition of mixing different musical styles to create a unique sound. Several other artists made guest appearances on the record, including rapper Mos Def, singer Macy Gray, and De La Soul, a group that has been an inspiration for the Peas. *Bridging the Gap* was critically acclaimed and received numerous award nominations, particularly for music video awards.

Fergie Joins the Group

The Black Eyed Peas had used back-up singers, notably singer Kim Hill, on their early releases. Hill decided to leave the Peas while the group was working on *Elephunk* in 2001. The group needed to find a singer for the female part in "Shut Up," a male/female duet about the end of a relationship. Fergie was introduced to the group by a mutual friend who thought she might do well with the Peas' freewheeling musical style. The Peas originally planned to have Fergie perform on just that one song, but she meshed so well with the others that they brought her in as a full-fledged Pea. Fergie jumped at the opportunity to join the dynamic group, seeing it as the creative outlet she needed and hadn't yet been able to find in her own music career.

With her performing history, previous experience singing with a band, multicultural background, and open-minded approach to making music, the other Peas thought that Fergie would fit right in. And, in fact, she did. "She's like a sister to us," said will. She soon put her talents to work on many of the album's hit songs, enabling the Peas to attract yet more fans. Despite the fun she has with the Peas, Fergie takes her job very seriously. She says, "I couldn't feel more blessed about the guys taking a chance and putting me in the band. I give 110 percent. This isn't some little cool cute thing I decided to do."

Elephunk

The Peas' third record, *Elephunk*, was released in 2003. "We liked the idea of an elephant meaning something which is strong and can be aggressive, although that isn't its nature," will said. "We wanted to bring in the idea of funk that isn't typical." And *Elephunk* was anything but typical, especially for hip-hop. It blended musical elements of Motown, heavy metal rock, Brazilian samba beats, Jamaican reggae, Middle Eastern sounds, and jazz. It quickly became a gold record, rising to No. 1 on the *Billboard* Top 40 chart and achieving platinum-plus sales.

"Where Is the Love," the Peas' first No. 1 hit song, was written, recorded, and produced with Justin Timberlake. The song is a response to the tragedies of September 11, 2001. As will explained, "9-11 opened our minds up and opened our eyes up. With 'Where Is the Love,' I think we're asking questions the whole world is asking. . . . The song is connecting [with people] because everyone can relate to it." After this successful collaboration, the Peas were invited to tour with Justin Timberlake and pop diva Christina Aguilera. That opportunity helped the Peas expand their fan base even more, and sales of *Elephunk* soared.

Several more songs from the record became hits and were recognized with industry awards. "Let's Get It Started" was awarded the 2004 Grammy for

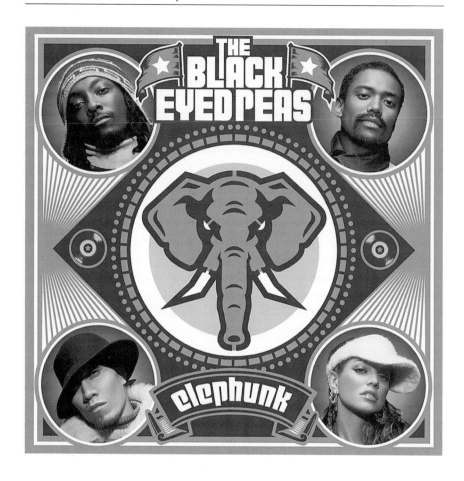

Best Rap Performance by a Duo or Group. "Hey Mama" won a 2004 MTV Video Music Award for Best Choreography. MTV also nominated the song for Best Hip-Hop Video and Best Dance Video that year.

Responding to Criticism

In the midst of the success of *Elephunk*, the Peas were also being harshly criticized by some of their long-time fans. The Peas were accused of "selling out" because they recorded and toured with Justin Timberlake and especially because they added Fergie to the group. Because Timberlake had been part of N'Sync, an all-male group that recorded pop tunes, he was dismissed by some Peas fans as being "too pop." Fergie had also recorded pop songs with Wild Orchid, but beyond that, some Peas fans saw her as lacking in hip-hop credibility and unworthy of being part of the Black Eyed Peas. *Vibe* reports that some fans were complaining that the Peas had become "too commercial" in their quest for hit records.

Fans posting on web site discussion boards were writing things like, "The Black Eyed Peas were dope before when they were underground, and before they got that girl." Fergie was very hurt by such comments. She felt that these fans weren't even giving her a chance. "I've had to prove myself show by show. . . . I cried a lot in the beginning," she admitted. "It was a big change for them. Certain fans from the underground scene didn't want to see their Black Eyed Peas change, and to a lot of people, it was my fault."

But will responded to these comments with surprise, saying, "And they call it a sell-out for what reason? Because we have a white girl in our group now? I don't think that just because one day you do a jazzy record and then you do a funky record, [doesn't] mean you sold out. It just means you like music and you're trying to dabble in every ray of color in the music world." The Peas insisted that adding Fergie to the group was not a calculated move to increase record sales. After Kim Hill left the group, they simply needed another female singer. "We had been hanging out with her a lot in 2002, and we just realized that Fergie had the same spirit as us," will explained. "What's more important—appeasing somebody else, or surrounding ourselves with talented [people]? We all knew the answer to that one." The phenomenal success of *Elephunk* proved that most fans agreed.

> "
>
> *"They call it a sell-out for what reason? Because we have a white girl in our group now? I don't think that just because one day you do a jazzy record and then you do a funky record, [doesn't] mean you sold out. It just means you like music and you're trying to dabble in every ray of color in the music world."*
>
> "

Monkey Business

After the release of *Elephunk*, the Peas went on tour for 18 months straight. will brought along a mobile recording studio, and *Monkey Business* was recorded all over the world—in airplanes, trains, hotel rooms, and anywhere else the group found themselves with some time to fill. Fergie recalled "It was hard for me to get used to writing and recording on the road, because usually I'm doing studio time all at once, and then touring all at once," Fergie recalled. "This way was a big challenge, but it turned out to be this creative waterfall which just fell down into the huge ocean of *Monkey Business*."

Monkey Business was the first album to be co-written by all four Peas. This produced a record that is musically diverse in the usual Peas way, but also includes some surprises. For example, on the track "Bebot," apl raps the

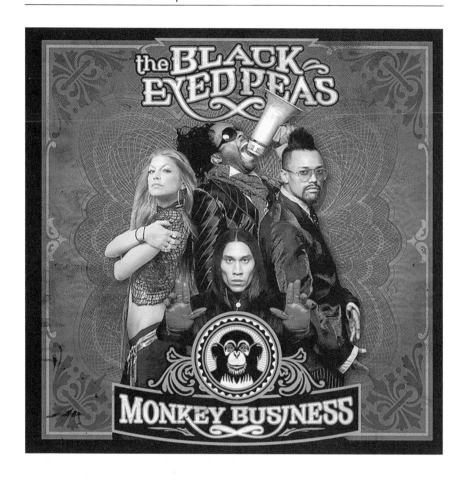

entire song in Tagalog, the language of his home province in the Philippines. "I'm proud of who I am, where I came from, what I was born into, and I would represent that till I die. As much as I could put into this business, I want to involve who I am and my culture." There are also guest spots by Justin Timberlake, British pop singer Sting, and godfather of soul James Brown. "*Monkey Business* is very much about the types of songs we play live. It's about a party," will said. "It's very much about us and the crowd on this record."

By 2004, *Monkey Business* had triple-platinum sales in Switzerland, Sweden, Germany, the United Kingdom, Australia, New Zealand, Canada and Singapore. The band has performed all over the world, including a tour stop in Vietnam, where they were the first American group to perform since 1972. "Don't Phunk With My Heart" was nominated for Best Group Video in the 2005 MTV Video Music Awards, and the Peas received two American

Music Awards in 2005, for Favorite Group in both the Pop/Rock and Rap/Hip-Hop categories.

Living with Fame

The runaway success of their last two records has resulted in lots of new opportunities for the Peas. Their music has been used in ads for Dr. Pepper, iPod, and Best Buy. "Let's Get It Started" has become a sports anthem for NBA basketball, and the Peas performed at the 2005 Super Bowl. "Everybody loves the Black Eyed Peas. The group is a social connector whose music bridges generations," said Tracy Perlman, director of entertainment marketing for the NFL. The Peas even appeared as characters in the computer game "Urbz: Sims in the City," for which they re-recorded some of their hits in Simlish, the language of the Sims world. They have continued to tour with diverse musicians, including the Dave Matthews Band, Cold Play, No Doubt, Metallica, Everclear, Blink-182, and the Rolling Stones. Their widespread appeal, according to will, is because the Peas love what they do. "I think the fact that we just have fun with music is the reason why it works for us. . . . It's really that simple." Taboo agreed, saying that "We make songs that can be understood by the normal listener. You don't have to be a part of the scene to understand what we're talking about."

> *Their widespread appeal, according to will, is because the Peas love what they do. "I think the fact that we just have fun with music is the reason why it works for us. . . . It's really that simple."*

Fame means that the Peas lead a busy public life on the road. They travel all over the world to perform in concerts and at other events. They participate in charity benefits and fundraisers, and are heavily involved in Rock the Vote, a political awareness group for young people. In between, they field media requests, appear at promotional events, and somehow find time to write and record new music. Taboo describes a typical day in the life of a Pea: "This is how my day goes. We perform at exactly 9:30 at night, get off the stage at about 10:40 p.m., then there's the after party at every city. We're at the after party until like 2 a.m. Then we get on the tour bus, drive for about six hours until we get to the next city, get to the hotel, lay down for a couple of hours, do phoners [phone interviews], and my whole day starts all over again."

But the Peas aren't complaining. All their hard work has begun to pay off, and they have big plans for the future. "We've all worked so long and hard for this,"

Fergie declared. "And we understand that it can go away, beause we've all tried things that have been less successful. We're definitely all still hungry."

HOME AND FAMILY

Little has been reported about the home lives of the group members. Perhaps because she is a favorite target of paparazzi and reporters, Fergie keeps quiet about her personal life. Taboo is a single father, raising his son Joshua, who was born in 1993. will admits to working all the time, while apl is planning to bring his family from the Philippines to the U.S.

——— *"* ———

Taboo describes a typical day in the life of the Black Eyed Peas: "We perform at exactly 9:30 at night, get off the stage at about 10:40 p.m., then there's the after party ... until like 2 a.m. Then we get on the tour bus, drive for about six hours until we get to the next city, get to the hotel, lay down for a couple of hours, do [phone interviews], and my whole day starts all over again."

——— *"* ———

HOBBIES AND OTHER INTERESTS

Although their busy schedule leaves little time for outside interests, the Peas still manage to pursue their own musical projects. Taboo, apl, and Fergie all plan to release solo albums. Taboo plans a Spanish-language record, apl wants to make a record of Filipino music, and Fergie is preparing an R&B record. will founded his own record label, the will.-i.am music group, and has already signed a contract with Fergie for her solo album. will has also teamed up with Justin Timberlake to form JAW Breakers, a record production company. will's entire life is music, and he has a reputation for being a workaholic. "When I go to sleep at 7 in the morning," he revealed, "there is still music playing in my head."

Movie projects are also in the works for some of the Peas. Taboo has a part in *Dirty*, an upcoming movie starring Cuba Gooding Jr. Meanwhile, Fergie is appearing in her first major movie with a part in *Poseidon*, a remake of the 1972 shipwreck disaster film *The Poseidon Adventure*. She will play a singer and perform two songs in the movie, one of which she co-wrote with will specifically for the film. And although apl doesn't have any plans to appear in a movie himself, a Filipino television station has produced a movie based loosely on his life.

The Peas are also involved in projects outside the entertainment industry. A former student at the Los Angeles Fashion Institute of Design and Merchandising, will established his i.am Clothing company and recently pre-

*The members of Black Eyed Peas: (from left) Taboo, will.i.am,
apl.de.ap, and Fergie.*

miered his line of women's and men's wear. Meanwhile, Taboo described himself as a dedicated shoe lover and confessed to owning more than 700 pairs. He buys them wherever the Peas travel on tour and jokes about opening his own shoe store someday. Taboo has also been active in philanthropic work; he is funding the development of a community center in his hometown of Rosemead, California.

SELECTED RECORDINGS

Behind the Front, 1998
Bridging the Gap, 2000
Elephunk, 2003
Monkey Business, 2005

HONORS AND AWARDS

Grammy Award: 2004, Best Rap Performance by a Duo or Group, for "Let's Get It Started"; 2006, Best Rap Performance By a Duo Or Group, for "Don't Phunk With My Heart"
American Music Awards: 2005, Favorite Pop/Rock Band, Duo or Group and Favorite Rap/Hip-Hop Band, Duo or Group
Patrick Lippert Award (Rock the Vote): 2005

FURTHER READING

Books

Contemporary Musicians, Vol. 45, 2004

Periodicals

Billboard, July 31, 2004, p.15
Cosmo Girl, Nov. 2004, p.138
Entertainment Weekly, May 27, 2005, p.44
Los Angeles Times, Feb. 4, 2001, p.8
Mix, June 1, 2004, p.7
Newsweek, May 16, 2005, p.66
San Francisco Chronicle, Aug. 8, 2005, p.C1
Seventeen, Sep. 2005, p.222
USA Today, June 9, 2005, p.D7
Vibe, July 2005, p.104

Online Articles

http://www.mtv.com/bands/b/black_eyed_peas/news_feature_053005
    (*MTV.com*, "Black Eyed Peas: Mad All Over the Place," May 27, 2005)
http://www.mtv.com/music/#/music/artist/black_eyed_peas/bio.jhtml
    (*MTV.com*, "Black Eyed Peas: Bio," undated)
http://www.rollingstone.com/artists/4522/biography
    (*RollingStone.com*, "Black Eyed Peas Biography," undated)

Online Databases

Biography Resource Center Online, 2006, article from *Contemporary Musicians*, 2004

ADDRESS

Black Eyed Peas
A&M Records
2220 Colorado Avenue
Santa Monica, CA 90404

WORLD WIDE WEB SITES

http://www.blackeyedpeas.com

Neda DeMayo 1960-

American Wildlife Conservationist
Founder of Return to Freedom—The American Wild
Horse Sanctuary

BIRTH

Neda DeMayo was born on January 20, 1960, in New Haven,
Connecticut. She is the daughter of William S. DeMayo, a financial consultant and professor at the University of New Haven, and his wife, Stella DeMayo. Neda has a sister, Diana.

YOUTH AND EDUCATION

DeMayo started taking riding lessons at the age of five in Hamden Connecticut. "I cannot remember a time when I did not love horses," she recalled. "One of my first words was 'horse.'" A defining moment in her life occurred at age six, when she first became aware of the U.S. Bureau of Land Management (BLM) policy of rounding up and capturing wild horses. "I can remember seeing wild horses on television being chased by everything from cowboys to hovering helicopters and wanting to help them escape and have a place for them to remain free, together, and safe," she said. "As I grew up, my relationship with horses deepened and I began to think about somehow, some way to start a sanctuary for wild horses."

When DeMayo was eight years old, her family moved to a home on four acres in the woods in Cheshire, Connecticut. She got a horse of her own— a black Morgan named Sam—and practically lived on his back. She and her friends rode their horses to the local Dairy Queen for ice cream, and to a nearby pond to go swimming. They even went camping by horseback on full moon nights.

> "I can remember seeing wild horses on television being chased by everything from cowboys to hovering helicopters and wanting to help them escape and have a place for them to remain free, together, and safe," DeMayo said.

After graduating from Hammonassett High School, DeMayo left Connecticut and headed west with her best friend and her dog. For the next few years, she traveled all over the world studying traditional healing methods and holistic medicine. In the mid 1980s she studied fashion design in San Francisco and eventually joined her sister in Los Angeles, where she also worked in the theater and film industry.

CAREER HIGHLIGHTS

Pursuing Her Childhood Dream

Living in California in the late 1980s, DeMayo worked as a holistic healing practitioner and also as a costume designer for theatrical productions. Within a few years she was serving as a fashion stylist for Hollywood stars, including Sandra Bullock, Antonio Banderas, and David Duchovny. In 1994, however, she was involved in two serious car accidents that made her reconsider her career path. "I realized that I was focused on a career and was always running to survive while holding the dream that one day I would buy a ranch and have a sanctuary for animals and humans. I needed to get clear about how I wanted to spend my time because you don't know how long your life is going to last."

Creating a sanctuary to protect wild horses was a long-time dream for DeMayo.

Remembering her childhood passion for horses—and especially her concern for wild horses—DeMayo began pursuing her lifelong dream of creating a horse sanctuary. Over the next few years, she visited existing wild-horse sanctuaries in North America. During this period she also learned about habitat conservation programs, worked with several nonprofit groups, and traveled around California and New Mexico searching for suitable land.

In the mid 1990s, DeMayo purchased an Arabian mare and re-entered the world of horses to study horse behavior and communication. She visited wild horses in a few locations and frequently brought friends to a sanctuary in Northern California. Her quest for knowledge also led her to trainer Carolyn Resnick. A famous "horse whisperer" who used leadership dynamics predicated on daily behavior and relationships in wild horse herds, Resnick followed an approach that was based on respect for the complex inner nature of horses. Upon visiting Resnick's ranch, DeMayo noticed that "There was an awakeness in the animals there, a spirit you don't find in most domesticated horses. . . . Her horses were free when they were with her."

Saving the Mustang

During her preparations for the launch of her wild-horse sanctuary, DeMayo learned a great deal about the history of horses in America. The modern horse evolved in North America about 1.6 million years ago. Early humans hunted the species to extinction on the continent, but horses were reintroduced by Spanish explorers in the late 1500s. Native Americans, early European farmers and settlers, and the U.S. Cavalry all domesticated horses for different uses over the next three centuries. Some of these horses escaped or were set free, and they adapted to the land and established wild herds. By 1900 around two million wild horses, or mustangs, roamed free in the United States. Due to habitat loss and government-sponsored capture and removal programs, however, the wild horse population has declined to only about 35,000 today. The remaining mustangs live in ten U.S. states, with the largest number in Nevada, followed by Wyoming, California, Oregon, Utah, and Arizona.

———— **"** ————

"The ancestors of these horses helped us build this country," said DeMayo. "They carried us across the land from east to west. They took us forward into battle; they pulled our plows; they drove our cattle. The horse holds a mythical status for Americans; he touches us deeply, symbolically, archetypically. He touches our hearts."

———— **"** ————

American wild horses received federal government protection in 1971 with the passage of the Wild Free-Roaming Horse and Burro Act, which gave the Bureau of Land Management responsibility for managing the herds. Calling mustangs "living symbols of the historic pioneer spirit of the west," the legislation said that the BLM could only remove wild horses and burros from public lands if the animals were overpopulating or causing habitat destruction. But the BLM faced a great deal of pressure from powerful ranchers and beef producers who wanted the horse herds removed so that they would have more public grazing land for their livestock. Over the years, the ranching interests succeeded in gradually weakening the protections—and reducing the amount of land—granted to mustangs. In order to keep wild horse numbers in check and ensure adequate grazing areas for cattle, the BLM held annual roundups and offered "excess" horses for adoption to private individuals.

DeMayo argued that wild horses deserve protection because of their important role in American history and culture, as well as their unique genetic and behavioral characteristics. The mustang "has earned special status by having woven himself into everything that is American," she stated. "The ancestors of these horses helped us build this country. They carried us across the land from east to west. They took us forward into battle; they pulled our plows; they drove our cattle. The horse holds a mythical status for Americans; he touches us deeply, symbolically, archetypically. He touches our hearts."

Preserving Horse Communities

In 1997, with the help of her parents and sister, DeMayo purchased a 300-acre ranch in the rolling hills of Lompoc, California, about 30 miles from Santa Barbara. She turned this property into Return to Freedom—The American Wild Horse Sanctuary. As she prepared to bring the first horses to the sanctuary, DeMayo decided to take a unique approach aimed at preserving entire herds of mustangs. In their natural environment, wild horses live in groups that work together like human families or communities. A mustang herd is typically led by a dominant male horse (called a stallion) with a lead mare. A herd also includes a number of adult female horses (mares), as well as younger horses of both sexes. BLM roundup and adoption programs often isolated individuals from their herds, causing deep trauma in captured horses and disrupted herds alike. DeMayo wanted to prevent that.

Beginning in 1998, Return to Freedom (RTF) became the new home of almost 200 wild horses in six herd groups. Some of the horses had been captured on the open range, like those DeMayo had seen on television as a child. Some had been rescued from horse auctions, where they might otherwise have been purchased by slaughterhouses. Others had been removed from adoptive homes after the owners decided that the animals could not be trained. "We have been able to relocate entire herds to RTF, where they are thriving because they are together in their natural family and social groups," DeMayo explained. "We have also been working with various experts on natural and non-intrusive population management programs so we don't have to separate the stallions from the herds. Return to Freedom has garnered support and interest as a model program because of our innovative approach to natural herd management."

DeMayo also decided to include an educational component to RTF. "I knew I had to educate because I knew I couldn't save every horse," she noted. "We recognize that, just as the earth has much to teach us about life, animals have much to teach us about living, communication, and instinct." RTF operates as a "living museum" that offers clinics, tours, and guided "wild horse walks" to the public in exchange for a small donation. The facility also invites groups of at-risk children—many of them from the inner city. At RTF, these kids get the opportunity to experience nature and learn compassion, trust, and confidence. No one is allowed to ride the mustangs that live at RTF. Instead, the horses roam freely with their herds, and DeMayo helps visitors observe and interact with the animals in their natural environment. "You don't have to ride a horse to have a relationship with it," she explained.

27

"Horse people—riders, breeders, trainers—who know far more about horses than I do, leave here in tears when they see wild horses living as they're meant to. They say, 'Oh my God, I never knew.'"

Providing a Home for Spirit

In 2002 RTF gained a famous resident when it was selected to be the permanent home of Spirit, the Kiger mustang stallion that served as the model for the main character in the animated film *Spirit: Stallion of the Cimarron*. The movie, which took four years to complete, was one of the most technically complex animated films of its time. It tells the story of Spirit's struggle to maintain his freedom during a period of rapid change and development in the Old West.

> "You don't have to ride a horse to have a relationship with it," DeMayo explained. "Horse people—riders, breeders, trainers—who know far more about horses than I do, leave [the sanctuary] in tears when they see wild horses living as they're meant to."

Once the movie was completed, the production company DreamWorks SKG searched the country for an appropriate home for the real-life mustang. "We were looking for two things: a place that had a philosophy we were comfortable with, and a location appropriate to the personality of Spirit," said Ann Daly, head of the feature animation department. "We felt we found it with the American Wild Horse Sanctuary. It allowed us to make a choice that's best for Spirit's personality and to extend the message of what the movie is about."

DeMayo praised the message of the film and expressed gratitude for the gift of the well-known horse. "Horses are a symbol of freedom and the American spirit, just like the bald eagle," she said. "In the animated movie *Spirit*, both animals travel across the plains side-by-side. That's why it was particularly thrilling that RTF was chosen ... to be the home of the horse that the movie's drawings, animation, and spirit were based on." Spirit has served as a sort of ambassador, bringing media attention, visitors, and donations to RTF. "They couldn't have picked a more perfect horse," DeMayo noted. "He's fun to be with. He has a wonderful temperament. He's beautiful. He's a great representation of the Kiger [breed]."

Fighting Political Battles

In addition to operating RTF, DeMayo has also been involved in political actions aimed at preserving the remaining mustangs in the United States.

DeMayo with Spirit, the Kiger mustang that served as the model for the animated movie hero.

Wild mustangs deserve our protection, according to DeMayo.

In the summer of 2004, RTF spearheaded the American Wild Horse Preservation Campaign (AWHPC) after she and a few colleagues rented a plane in Nevada and investigated a few herd management areas. These are areas where captured animals are kept. What they saw was disappointing and confirmed their suspicions. The AWHPC was created as a campaign supported by a coalition of organizations.

Then in November 2004, U.S. Senator Conrad Burns of Montana quietly added an amendment to a major Congressional spending bill that overturned many of the protections that wild horses had enjoyed for 34 years. The Burns Amendment allowed captured wild horses to be sold for commercial purposes, including slaughter. Previously, the BLM was required to place these animals in adoptive homes, and the private owners were required to keep them for at least one year before transferring ownership. Senator Burns argued that his amendment was necessary because it cost the government $19 million per year to keep thousands of mustangs in long-term holding facilities. He claimed that the new rule only applied to horses that were not considered adoptable because they were over ten years old or had already been offered for adoption three times.

Immediately after passage of the Burns Amendment, the coalition of wildlife conservation and environmental organizations supporting the American Wild Horse Preservation Campaign numbered 25 groups and represented over 10 million Americans nationwide. This coalition tried to raise public awareness of the need to preserve wild horses and their habitat and fought for new laws to protect the remaining mustangs. DeMayo and others in the campaign claimed that the Burns Amendment was a poorly disguised attempt to dispose of wild horses that should have been allowed to remain in the wild. The urgency of the situation became clear in the spring of 2005, when 41 wild horses that had been purchased under the Burns Amendment were slaughtered and turned into meat products for sale in Europe. Horse meat is a standard food in some European countries.

In November 2005 DeMayo and other mustang supporters won passage of an amendment that prevented the slaughter of American horses—both wild and domestic—for one year. The legislation prohibited meat inspectors from the U.S. Department of Agriculture (USDA) from working at horse slaughterhouses. Since all meat must be inspected by the USDA before it can be exported to foreign countries (and horse meat is not consumed in the United States), the bill effectively shut down all horse-slaughtering operations in America.

——— " ———

"They're not asking for much," DeMayo said of the last mustangs. "You can't look at their numbers and say they're a nuisance out there. They're just not making anyone any money. I think they belong to the American people, because they represent us out there. They are the American spirit."

——— " ———

DeMayo has also worked toward finding a solution that will allow wild mustangs to remain on public lands. She and other experts dismiss claims from ranching interests that wild mustangs are too hard on the land. In fact, they argue that horses provide valuable ecological benefits to the land by improving the soil and reseeding native plants with their manure. DeMayo also asserts that the four million privately owned cattle that range across public lands do far more environmental damage than 35,000 wild horses. "They're not asking for much," she said of the last mustangs. "You can't look at their numbers and say they're a nuisance out there. They're just not making anyone any money. I think they belong to the American people, because they represent us out there. They are the American spirit."

Planning for the Future

Today, DeMayo is nationally recognized as an expert in wild horse behavior and non-invasive horse-handling methods. RTF serves as home to 220 animals, and the operation includes six full-time staff members in addition to

DeMayo and her family. It costs about $35,000 per month to run the sanctuary, and much of this funding comes from grants, private donations, and free services from veterinarians and other professionals. DeMayo hopes to acquire more land to expand the sanctuary in the near future. "I didn't want to run a little rescue operation," she noted. "I wanted to create a way of preserving these horses over the long term."

——— " ———

"Human beings have a tendency to see the natural world as a threat, as something they need to conquer, enhance, or profit from," DeMayo said. "In the process, we often destroy the things we love and the things we need.... I believe we have a responsibility to maintain a healthy balance between our desires and the needs of other creatures and the environment."

——— " ———

Toward this end, DeMayo is working hard to establish The American Wild Horse Conservancy— the next step for Return to Freedom. A historical land trust, the conservancy would be a large scale wildlife preserve that would integrate wild horses as a wildlife species and maintain them in genetically viable herd groups.

DeMayo and RTF have attracted the support of a number of prominent horse lovers, including actress and singer Hilary Duff, star of the TV series "Lizzie McGuire," and actor Viggo Mortensen, star of the hit films *Hidalgo* and *The Lord of the Rings* trilogy. Another supporter was John Fusco, the mustang preservationist and screenwriter *(Spirit: Stallion of the Cimarron, Hidalgo)*, who aligned with Return to Freedom's efforts to establish the conservancy. Actor Robert Redford also lent his powerful name to the cause, drafting a letter to members of Congress in support of legislation that would ban the slaughter of wild horses.

Through her work with wild horses, DeMayo tries to help people understand the importance of preserving wildness in the world. "Human beings have a tendency to see the natural world as a threat, as something they need to conquer, enhance, or profit from," she said. "In the process, we often destroy the things we love and the things we need. As stewards of this world, I believe we have a responsibility to maintain a healthy balance between our desires and the needs of other creatures and the environment."

MARRIAGE AND FAMILY

While traveling in Europe in the early 1980s, DeMayo met a Dutch man with whom she was involved for 11 years. The couple traveled between

Europe and America for a few years and settled in California. They were married for five years, but have since divorced. DeMayo lives in a house on the Return to Freedom sanctuary in Lompoc, California. Her parents moved to another house on the ranch and her sister lives with her family in Van Nuys, California. They are all actively involved in the project.

FURTHER READING

Books

Rappaport, Jill, and Wendy Wilkinson. *People We Know, Horses They Love*, 2004
Resnick, Carolyn. *Naked Liberty*, 2005

Periodicals

California Riding, May 2005, p.56
Lifetime Magazine, Sep. 2004, p.111
Los Angeles Times, July 20, 2001, Southern California Living, p.1
People, May 9, 2005, p.219
Santa Barbara (CA) News-Press, June 12, 2002, p.B1
Santa Maria (CA) Times, June 22, 2002, p.C5
Teen Newsweek, Feb. 15, 2005, p.7
Young Rider, May/June 2004

Online Articles

http://www.californiaheartland.org/archive/hl_641/horsesanctuary.htm
(*California Heartland*, "Program 641: Horse Sanctuary," undated)
http://news.nationalgeographic.com/news/2001/10/1024_
TVmustangs.html
(*National Geographic News*, "U.S. Wild Horses: Too Many Survivors on Too Little Land?" Oct. 26, 2001)

ADDRESS

Neda DeMayo
Return to Freedom
P.O. Box 926
Lompoc, CA 93438

WORLD WIDE WEB SITES

http://www.returntofreedom.org
http://www.wildhorsepreservation.com
http://www.dreamworks.com/spirit

GREEN DAY

**William (Billie Joe) Armstrong 1972-
Michael Pritchard (Mike Dirnt) 1972-
Frank Edwin Wright III (Tré Cool) 1972-**
American Punk Rock Band
Creators of the Hit Records *Dookie* and
American Idiot

EARLY YEARS

Green Day is a three-man punk rock group whose members include Billie Joe Armstrong (lead singer and guitarist), Mike Dirnt (bassist), and Tré Cool (drummer).

Billie Joe Armstrong

William (Billie Joe) Armstrong was born on February 17, 1972, in Rodeo, California. He is the youngest of six children. His father, Andy, was a truck driver and jazz drummer in his spare time. His mother, Ollie, was a waitress at Rod's Hickory Pit, a local roadside diner.

Even as a young child, Armstrong enjoyed singing and performing. When he was only five years old, he would perform for patients in children's hospitals and for residents of nursing homes. "Music has always been in my household," he remembered, "whether it was my dad playing jazz or my sister playing clarinet or something like that." During an interview with MTV, Armstrong said that he watched the Ramones' film called *Rock 'n' Roll High School* when he was nine years old. "To me, what I saw was the perfect rock band," he recalled. "They had songs that just stuck in your head. Just like a hammer, they banged right into your brain." By the time he was 15, Armstrong could play the guitar, piano, drums, harmonica, mandolin, and saxophone.

—— " ——

"Music has always been in my household," Armstrong remembered, "whether it was my dad playing jazz or my sister playing clarinet or something like that."

—— " ——

When Billie Joe was just ten years old, Andy Armstrong died of cancer of the upper digestive tract, which had spread through the rest of his body. Billie Joe and his father had a very close relationship. He recalls, "Only a few days before he drew his last breath, he gave me my first guitar. I gave it a name—Blue—because it was a blue Fender Stratocaster copy. It ended up battered, covered in duct tape and stickers, because I played it so much. It's become my trademark, and I still use replicas on stage and in videos."

After Andy died, Ollie had to struggle to make ends meet. She continued to work at the diner, but other things changed for the worse. Billie Joe's sister, Anna, confided in an interview, "Our family changed a lot because my parents had been very kid oriented. And all of a sudden, my mother withdrew and threw herself into waitressing. The family structure broke up. Then my mom remarried about a year or two afterward, and that was a big change for the negative." One positive in all this was his friendship with Mike Dirnt, who became his best friend.

On the day before his 18th birthday, Armstrong dropped out of high school. He decided that the demanding schedule of his music career should take precedence over his education.

Green Day in New York City in 1994.

Mike Dirnt

Mike Dirnt was born Michael Pritchard on May 4, 1972, in Rodeo, California. His birth mother was a heroine addict at the time of his birth. She gave Dirnt up for adoption when he was a baby. His adoptive father was white, and his adoptive mother was Native American. They divorced when he was seven years old. For a while, Dirnt divided his time between both parents' homes. After several confrontations with his father, he finally settled in with his mother. They lived in conditions barely above poverty level. "When I was in fourth or fifth grade, my mom stayed out all night, came home the next day with a guy, and he moved in," Dirnt said. "I'd never met the guy before, and all of a sudden he's my stepdad." Initially he did not get along with his new stepfather. But the two eventually developed a very close relationship and remained close until his stepfather passed away when Dirnt was 17.

Dirnt used to play guitar, playing with his friend Billie Joe Armstrong. But then one day his friend's brother told him that no matter how many guitar players there are in a band, there would be only one bass player. That's when Dirnt said, "Bingo!" His mom bought him an old bass from a pawn shop. It was not in good condition, but it worked. According to Dirnt, "It had buttons all over it and two flat-wound strings: E and A. But the bass made the right sounds, so I could have band practice. Billie and I would just plug into the same amp and play all night."

When Dirnt was 15 years old, his mother moved out of the area. He didn't want to move with her, so he moved out on his own. After living out of his truck for a while, he rented a room in Armstrong's house. Dirnt worked as a busboy and a cook to earn money to support himself.

Although Armstrong dropped out of high school, Dirnt continued and graduated. He is the only one of the three band members to graduate from high school. He did take a few college courses but never received his college degree.

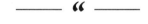

"It had buttons all over it and two flat-wound strings: E and A," Dirnt said about his first bass guitar. "But the bass made the right sounds, so I could have band practice. Billie and I would just plug into the same amp and play all night."

Tré Cool

Tré Cool was born Frank Edwin Wright III in Germany on December 9, 1972. His father had been a helicopter pilot in Vietnam. When he returned to the United States, the family moved to Willits, California, which is in a very remote area in the Mendocino Mountains. Cool's father, Frank Wright II, worked as a builder, bus driver, and trucking company owner. His mother, Linda, was a bookkeeper.

When Cool was in second grade, he learned to play the violin. He later switched to drums, which Linda said was "pretty noisy, but a definite improvement on the violin." Luckily the noise didn't bother the Wrights' closest neighbor, who lived a mile away. That neighbor, Lawrence Livermore, was the leader of a band called The Lookouts. Livermore was also a writer for *Maximum RockNRoll*, a San Francisco punk rock publication, and he later founded Lookout! Records. As there wasn't much to do in Willits, Cool started to hang out with Livermore, who eventually asked him to join The Lookouts as their drummer. Cool was just 12 years old.

Cool was class president in high school, but he eventually dropped out to pursue his music career. For a time after Cool joined Green Day, his dad drove the band around. His mother, Linda, recalled that "We always fretted when they went far from home. Frank wanted to be sure they had a good driver."

FORMING THE BAND

Both Armstrong and Dirnt grew up in Rodeo, California, which is approximately 15 miles north of Berkeley. The community in which they lived was mostly blue-collar. They were surrounded by large chemical refineries and oil refineries. Their hometown was "the most unscenic place on the planet," Armstrong once said. "We went to this elementary school, and they used to always send kids home with headaches. They figured it was because of the toxins that the refineries were throwing in the air."

Armstrong and Dirnt met when they were 11 years old and became fast friends. They shared an interest in music. They listened to and played music together, Armstrong on vocals and guitar and Dirnt on bass. There were no record stores in their town, so new music was hard to come by. "If you wanted to hear music, you had to play it [yourself]," Dirnt said. The two performed for other people any chance they had, in nearby cafes, at parties, and at friends' homes. They were not paid for these performances.

The two best friends began to hang out at the Gilman Street Project in Berkeley, a weekend underground punk club. The business was actually a caning and wicker shop by day, but it was a very well known destination for punk rockers on weekends. The club was started by a group of volunteers to encourage creativity in a violence-free environment. The non-profit club was open to the public of all ages. They did not sell alcohol, but it was not uncommon to see people drinking outside the club. According to Armstrong, "That place and that culture saved my life. It was like a gathering of outcasts and freaks."

In 1987, Armstrong and Dirnt formed a band called Sweet Children. They recruited drummer John Kiffmeyer to join their band. Kiffmeyer used the stage name Al Sobrante, a play on the name of his hometown, El Sobrante. The group made their debut performance at Rod's Hickory Pit, where Armstrong's mother worked as a waitress and Dirnt worked as a bus boy. Owner Richard Cotton said, "Billie Joe was a good kid. He used to sing and dance for our old folk in the banquet room. I remember telling Ollie, 'I'm going to see this kid in lights one day.'"

One other very significant performance, although they didn't know it at the time, was at a high school party where they played with another local band,

The Lookouts. The leader of the other band was Lawrence Livermore, and the drummer was Tré Cool. The performance itself was not a major event—there were only about five people there—but they played their hearts out. Livermore recalled that Sweet Children "played to those five kids as if they were the Beatles at Shea Stadium. It was only their third or fourth show ever, but I said right then that I was going to make a record with these guys."

BECOMING GREEN DAY

Sweet Children started to perform at the Gilman Street Project in 1988. They played a handful of shows through the end of March 1989 and began to develop a following in the local punk scene. They played their last Gilman Project show as Sweet Children on April 1, 1989. Later that month, they changed their name to Green Day. By that time, they were working with Lawrence Livermore and Lookout! Records to release their first EP.

Green Day released a four-song EP entitled *1,000 Hours* under the Lookout! label. They continued to play as many gigs as they could get. They played at the Gilman Project under their new name for the first time on May 28, 1989. They became regulars there, performing on a monthly basis. They played with The Lookouts again in June 1989 for an audience of 1,300 at Veterans Hall in Garberville, California. In July 1990, Livermore and the rest of The Lookouts disbanded. Meanwhile, the members of Green Day—Armstrong, Dirnt, and Sobrante—worked odd jobs and played as stand-ins for other bands in order to earn money for their emerging band.

——— " ———

"The first time I ever saw Tré was when I went to see The Lookouts and I was outside ... with these girls," *Armstrong recalled. "Tré was walking by wearing a weird, old man's plaid suit—none of which was color-coordinated whatsoever—and an old bathing cap. These girls were like, 'Oh, The Lookouts!' And Tré just kind of turned to them and bowed. I remember thinking that was pretty cool."*

——— " ———

CAREER HIGHLIGHTS

Toward the end of 1989, Green Day and Lookout! Records decided that it was time to record a full-length album. For 22 hours, starting on December 29, 1989, the band recorded a 10-track album and called it *39/Smooth*. It cost them a total of $600 to record the album, which was released in 1990.

The cover of the CD Dookie, Green Day's *first big success.*

In April 1990, Green Day recorded a four-song EP titled *Slappy*. The band decided it was time to tour the United States, so they toured through the end of summer. At the end of the tour, Sobrante decided to quit the band and go to college. That left Green Day without a drummer, so Armstrong and Dirnt asked Tré Cool to join the group. As Armstrong recalled, "The first time I ever saw Tré was when I went to see The Lookouts and I was outside . . . with these girls. And Tré was walking by wearing a weird, old man's plaid suit—none of which was color-coordinated whatsoever—and an old bathing cap. These girls were like, 'Oh, The Lookouts!' And Tré just kind of turned to them and bowed. I remember thinking that was pretty cool."

In November 1990, the new Green Day set off for a 64-day European tour. They were one of five bands touring together. The band was still struggling financially at that time; they didn't even have their own equipment, so they borrowed where they could. "It made us a really good band," Armstrong said, "playing on different equipment and in different situations. I think it made us better because obviously there's a language difference and it meant we had to be more animated and project a bit more physically. We seemed to get a good response because we were so different from most of the bands playing."

When they returned from their European tour, they were ready to get serious. Cool's dad, Frank Wright II, fixed up an old bookmobile to serve as the band's tour bus. He built equipment racks and sleeping quarters on the bus. Also in 1991, Lookout! put the *39/Smooth* album together with *Slappy* on one album and released it as *1039/Smoothed Out Slappy Hours*.

Kerplunk

In 1992, with Cool as their new drummer, Green Day released the album *Kerplunk* under the Lookout! label. The album was an immediate success, breaking sales records for Lookout! The band toured extensively in North America and Europe, stopping in the United Kingdom, Germany, Czechoslovakia, Holland, Italy, and Poland. Through the tours, the band got their name out, and their popularity continued to grow. Several major record labels started to pay attention to this three-man punk band from California.

Critic Michael Baker described Dookie *as "a hot slice of straight-ahead snarl-pop, each of the 14 songs created according to Billie's maxim—'short, catchy, and in your face, so you'll want to hear it again.'"*

In 1993, Green Day and Lookout! parted on friendly terms. The band signed on with Reprise Records, a subsidiary of Warner Brothers. In their contract with Reprise, however, they did make sure that Lookout! Records retained all rights to their early recordings, including *Kerplunk*.

Dookie

In 1994, Green Day released *Dookie*. The music continued the punk sound from the group's earlier releases, what critic Michael Baker described as "a hot slice of straight-ahead snarl-pop, each of the 14 songs created according to Billie's maxim—'short, catchy, and in your face, so you'll want to hear it again.'" That view was echoed by music reviewer Christopher John Farley. "Bad attitudes often make for good rock 'n' roll," Farley wrote. "Green Day takes its adolescent snottiness and channels it into music. The result is a cathartic punk explosion and the best rock CD of the year so far.

This is music for people with raging hormones and short attention spans.... Every song on *Dookie* is brief and hard—the entire 14-track album is just 39 minutes long. Most of the songs are built around seductive guitar riffs, and each one is performed with controlled frenzy. The lyrics are about being young and screwed-up, about having your hopes and dreams dipped in disillusionment and then swallowed whole like so many Chicken McNuggets.... Green Day's punk nihilism works because it's delivered with self-deprecating humor, not with narcissistic rock angst."

> ————— " —————
>
> *"Bad attitudes often make for good rock 'n' roll," wrote music reviewer Christopher John Farley. "Green Day takes its adolescent snottiness and channels it into music. The result is [Dookie], a cathartic punk explosion and the best rock CD of the year so far. This is music for people with raging hormones and short attention spans."*
>
> ————— " —————

Dookie was a huge smash for the young group. The album debuted on the *Billboard* album charts at No. 127 and eventually reached No. 2 on the charts. They recorded a video for the first single on the album, "Longview," which fueled its popularity. *Dookie* reached platinum status ten times over by selling over 10 million copies.

On August 13 and 14, 1994, a two-day concert event called Woodstock II was held in Saugerties, New York, to commemorate the 25th anniversary of the original 1969 Woodstock event. Approximately 250,000 tickets were sold to the show in Saugerties, and Green Day was scheduled to perform on the afternoon of August 14. As the day went on, Green Day fans started to become impatient to see them. They booed other artists as they performed and chanted for Green Day. The event organizers finally started to announce, "Green Day will be on when their turn comes; please give these musicians their turn." By the time it was Green Day's turn to perform, things had started to get out of control. Fans threw mud everywhere, including on stage, and a huge mud fight broke out. The band tried to play, but their instruments were covered in mud, and the fans were wild. They finally had to be air lifted off the stage. By that time, Dirnt's front teeth had been shattered by security guards because he was so covered in mud that they couldn't tell him from the wild fans that had hopped on stage. "It was the closest thing to anarchy I've ever seen in my life, and I didn't like it," Armstrong admitted.

Making It in the Big Time

It was clear that Green Day's fan base was growing—and growing fast. Their songs appealed to people of all ages. Parents and kids could listen to their

Green Day performing in 2004.

music together, although some of their songs contain rather graphic language and the subject matter may not be appropriate for young kids. However, their songs were being played on radio stations with a variety of formats, including top 40, adult pop, modern rock, and hard rock. Their picture appeared on the covers of several music magazines. Part of Green Day's appeal has been that they are polite, articulate, and all-around good guys. They have even made every effort to keep ticket and merchandise prices low for their fans.

However, while the crossover appeal and the move to a big record label were great news for the band, many of their hardcore punk fans accused them of selling out. Few other punk bands ever made it big enough to move up as Green Day was doing. Dirnt responded to this accusation by saying, "Selling out is compromising your musical intentions, and we don't know how to do that." However, they found that they were no longer welcome at the Gilman Street Project, where their careers had begun.

Trying to Stay on Top

Green Day continued to tour. In October 1995, they released their next album, titled *Insomniac*. It debuted at No. 2 on Billboard's album charts and reached double platinum status. *Spin* magazine voted it No. 15 out of 20 of the best albums of 1995. Still, some critics were not as impressed with this album as they had been with the group's previous release.

The band had scheduled a European tour for 1996, but they unexpectedly cancelled, saying that they were too exhausted. They spent the next year

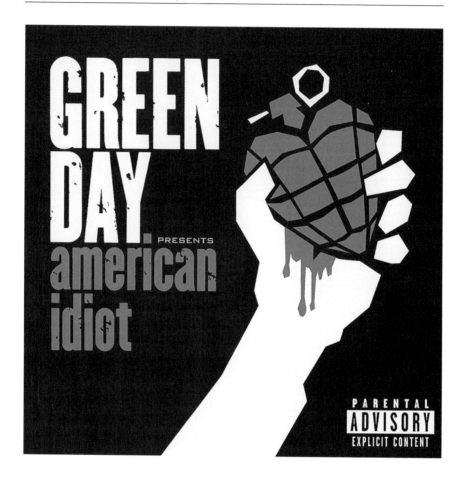

resting and writing new material for their next album, *Nimrod,* which was released in 1997. *Nimrod* reached only No. 10 on the charts.

For the next three years, Green Day took more time off. They released their next album, *Warning,* in 2000. This album did not hit the charts like their earlier albums. Some critics started to think that Green Day's popularity was coming to an end. Shortly thereafter, in 2001, they released a compilation album titled *International Superhits!* It included many of their previously released songs. The album topped out at No. 40 on the charts and went gold. The following year, Green Day released *Shenanigans,* another compilation album that included some of their less popular previously recorded songs.

Working Out Their Differences

Perhaps one reason for Green Day's declining popularity was the tension that had been building among the members. For three years after the release of *Warning*, the group did not talk about things for fear of "rocking the boat." By 2001, Dirnt admitted, "breaking up was an option. We were arguing a lot and we were miserable. We needed to shift directions." Things had gotten so bad that Armstrong was afraid to show the other two his new songs. He was afraid that they would immediately criticize him.

Armstrong finally realized that "to be the greatest band in the world, we would have to work on the small stuff." In 2003, the band got together to make a new record. At Armstrong's suggestion, the band agreed that once a week, they would start their daily band practice with conversation. Dirnt said, "We bared our souls to one another." Cool added, "Admitting we cared for each other was a big thing. We didn't hold anything back." At 31, Armstrong realized that it was time to grow up. "I felt like I was too old to be angry anymore," he said. "I didn't want to come across as the angry older guy. It's sexy to be an angry young man, but to be a bitter old [man] is another thing altogether."

This seemed to work for the band. Within five months, the band had recorded 20 new songs. Then one day the band came in to find that the master for these 20 tracks had been stolen. The master has not yet been recovered. While the band was furious at this discovery, it forced them to start from scratch. Armstrong headed to New York, leaving his family and the other band members for a month. He told *Rolling Stone*, "I was searching for something. I'm not sure it was the most successful trip." He spent a lot of time thinking and questioning himself.

—— ——

"We were in the studio watching the journalists embedded with the troops [during the Iraq War], and it was the worst version of reality television," Armstrong recalled. "Switch the channel, and it's Nick and Jessica. Switch, and it's 'Fear Factor.' Switch, and people are having surgery to look like Brad Pitt.... It's a sign of the times."

—— 99 ——

American Idiot

After Armstrong returned from New York, the group found the theme for their next album while watching television footage of U.S. troops invading Iraq. "We were in the studio watching the journalists embedded with the troops, and it was the worst version of reality television," Armstrong recalled. "Switch the channel, and it's Nick and Jessica. Switch, and it's 'Fear Factor.' Switch, and people are having surgery to look like Brad Pitt. . . . It's a sign of the times." After this experience, the group decided that the album would have a political theme.

Armstrong came up with the idea of writing a rock opera. The other two loved the idea, and they decided to call it *American Idiot*. Together, they worked on the story line, pushing to make it both a more personal and a more political album than their earlier releases. On *American Idiot*, the group was very critical of President George W. Bush and his political decisions. "The atmosphere can be anti-Bush, and I definitely had that in mind, but when you get down to it, it's a human story," Armstrong explained. "This album is about feelings. I didn't want to make a Rage against the Machine record. I wanted to make an album of heartfelt songs."

> "[What most fans] seem to be connecting with is the irresistible passion, intensity, and hookiness of the music," said reviewer Tom Sinclair. "And **Idiot's** brash sound has done more than just connect with the public. It's also struck a decisive blow for rock music—make that loud, butt-kickin' rock music, the kind that shakes your nerves and rattles your brain."

"The statement that we're making is that this is a pretty serious time," Armstrong said. "There are a lot of people living in fear, and people need something to relate to. This album is a reflection of what's going on." The song "Holiday" has very strong anti-war sentiments, while "Boulevard of Broken Dreams" talks about loneliness and disillusionment. Another popular song on the album was "Wake Me Up When September Comes." While the video for the song depicts a young man going off to war to provide for his lover, the song was really written by Armstrong about his father's death. "It's a song about how I watched my dad die," he admitted. "I had no problem letting the director turn my song into an anti-war statement. But the truth is, it's about my dad." According to reviewer Doug Small, "The album explores the confusion in an America split right down the middle politically, and the need to find one's individuality once again in the midst of too much information."

But *American Idiot* was not just a political statement—it was a record, too, that showed a variety of musical inspirations. "I used everything I knew about music," Armstrong revealed. "Show tunes, musicals like *Grease*, and the struggle between right and wrong, *The Joshua Tree* [by U2]—I tried to soak in everything and make it Green Day." That mix of musical sounds was

The members of Green Day: (from left) Mike Dirnt,
Billie Joe Armstrong, and Tré Cool.

a big advantage to reviewer Matt Hendrickson, who wrote that "The sound of *American Idiot* careens from old-school punk to Motown soul and Who-style anthems."

And ultimately, it was the music that captured its many fans, according to reviewer Tom Sinclair. "What most fans—Democrats, Republicans, and anarchists alike—seem to be connecting with is the irresistible passion, intensity, and hookiness of the music, all of which had been in short supply on the band's last two albums," wrote Sinclair. "And *Idiot's* brash sound has done more than just connect with the public. It's also struck a decisive blow for rock music—

make that loud, butt-kickin' rock music, the kind that shakes your nerves and rattles your brain."

Green Day debuted *American Idiot* in its entirety on September 16, 2004, in a live concert at Hollywood's Henry Fonda Music Box Theatre. It was an immediate success. *American Idiot* debuted at No. 1 on Billboard's album chart and remained in the top 10 for over a year. In 2005, the album was nominated for seven Grammy Awards, including Best Rock Album of the Year and Record of the Year. It won the award for Best Rock Album of the Year. Also in 2005, Green Day won four MTV Video Music Awards—Video of the Year, Best Group Video, Viewers' Choice Award, and Best Rock Video—for "Boulevard of Broken Dreams." This video has also won awards for best cinematography, best direction, and best editing. Then, in 2006, Green Day won another Grammy Award for another song from *American Idiot*, "Boulevard of Broken Dreams," which won the award for Record of the Year.

—————— " ——————

"We've been together for 15 years," said Cool. "For a marriage to last that long is an achievement. And that's only two people. This is three!"

—————— " ——————

With the success of *American Idiot*, Green Day proved to the world that they still had it. As Dirnt declared, "Ten years ago, a lot of people [wrote us off]. 'That's just a snotty little band from the Bay Area.' But we're a career band. And this album is a testament to what we perceive to be a great career." Cool added, "We've been together for 15 years. For a marriage to last that long is an achievement. And that's only two people. This is three!"

MARRIAGE AND FAMILY

Armstrong met his wife, Adrienne Nesser, during Green Day's first tour. They lost touch for about a year but eventually met up again and were married in 1994. They have two sons, Joseph Marciano, born in 1995, and Jakob Danger, born in 1998. Billie Joe and Adrienne are co-owners of Adeline Records, a small independent label.

Mike married his longtime girlfriend, Anastasia, in 1996. They have a daughter, Estelle Desiree, born in 1997. Mike and Anastasia divorced but remain on friendly terms. Dirnt remarried in 2004. He is currently a co-owner of Rudy's Can't Fail Café in Emeryville, California.

Tré Cool married Lisa Lyons in 1995. They have a daughter, Ramona, who was born earlier that year. The two divorced, and Cool remarried in 2000.

He and his second wife, Claudia, had a son named Frankito in 2001. Tré and Claudia divorced in 2003.

RECORDINGS

1039 / Smoothed Out Slappy Hours, 1991
Kerplunk, 1992
Dookie, 1994
Insomniac, 1995
Nimrod, 1997
Warning, 2000
American Idiot, 2004

HONORS AND AWARDS

Grammy Award: 1994, for Best Alternative Music Performance, for *Dookie*; 2005, for Best Rock Album, for *American Idiot*; 2006, for Record of the Year, for "Boulevard of Broken Dreams"
MTV Video Music Awards: 2005 (four awards), Video of the Year, Best Group Video, Viewers' Choice Award, and Best Rock Video, for "Boulevard of Broken Dreams"

FURTHER READING

Books

Contemporary Musicians, Vol. 40, 2003
Small, Doug. *Omnibus Press Presents the Story of Green Day*, 2005

Periodicals

Current Biography Yearbook, 2005
Entertainment Weekly, Feb. 11, 2005, p.26
Minneapolis Star Tribune, Sep. 16, 2005, p.E1
Rolling Stone, Feb. 24, 2005, p.40

Online Articles

http://www.freep.com
(*Detroit Free Press*, "Green Day's Story: 14 years, 7 discs," Sep. 9, 2005)

Online Databases

Biography Resource Center Online, 2006, *Contemporary Musicians*, 2003

ADDRESS

Green Day
Reprise Records
3300 Warner Boulevard
Burbank, CA 91505

WORLD WIDE WEB SITES

http://www.greenday.com
http://www.mtv.com/bands/az/green_day/bio.jhtml

Freddie Highmore 1992-
English Actor
Star of the Movies *Charlie and the Chocolate Factory*
and *Finding Neverland*

BIRTH

Freddie Highmore was born on February 14, 1992, in London, England. His father, Edward Highmore, is an actor. His mother is a prominent film talent agent. Her job is to find work and negotiate good pay and conditions for her actor clients. Highmore has a younger brother, Bertie.

YOUTH AND EDUCATION

Highmore's acting career began at about the same time that he began school, so he has had a lot of unusual childhood experiences. But he stresses that when he's not on the set of a movie, his daily life is much the same as that of other kids his age. "I try to stay a normal boy as much as possible," he said. "My friends think it's pretty cool that I've done one or two films. They don't treat me any differently."

In the fall of 2005 Highmore entered the equivalent of U.S. eighth grade. "When I am not filming, I go to a normal, local school [in north London]," he said. "While working I have a tutor, but I still follow the same curriculum as my school." Highmore is particularly good at foreign language classes. He is most fluent in Latin, but he also enjoys French and Spanish.

"I try to stay a normal boy as much as possible," Highmore said. *"My friends think it's pretty cool that I've done one or two films. They don't treat me any differently."*

CAREER HIGHLIGHTS

With two parents in show business, acting was a natural choice for Highmore. "I started doing little parts on television," he said. "People thought I wasn't too bad, and so I got offered bigger roles." He made his first film appearance at age six, playing the son of a woman played by English actress Helena Bonham Carter, in *Women Talking Dirty* (1999).

Highmore took minor roles in several other movies over the next few years. Then, in 2004, he appeared with the noted English actor Kenneth Branagh in *Five Children and It*. In this film, Highmore and several other children befriend an ancient, cranky sand fairy. The fairy grants them a wish each day. But the children learn that magic can be a messy and dangerous force.

Growing Acclaim

That same year, Highmore secured his first major film role, sharing the screen with twin tiger cubs in the movie *Two Brothers*. He played Raoul, the son of a French administrator in Southeast Asia in the 1920s. After the cubs are cruelly separated, Raoul receives one as a gift. He is certain that he can domesticate the wild animal. But he is forced to give up his beloved pet after it ravages his parents' house and attacks the family dog. Later, the grown cubs are pitted against each other by their human owners in a contest in which they are expected to fight to the death. But the brothers recognize each other despite their long separation and refuse to fight. Eventually, the brothers escape the clutches of their human captors and disappear into the wild together.

The movie was made by Jean-Jacques Annaud, who had a hit in 1988 with *The Bear*. Filmed in Cambodia and Thailand, *Two Brothers* won praise for

A scene from Finding Neverland.

its vibrant wildlife photography. But a number of reviewers dismissed the story line as predictable and superficial, and Highmore and the other human actors did not attract much notice.

Finding Neverland

Highmore received much more acclaim for his next role, in *Finding Neverland* (2004). His breakthrough performance won him wide recognition and the highest critical praise. The film is loosely based on the life of the famous author J.M Barrie, who was played by Johnny Depp. It explores how Barrie's friendship with four fatherless brothers inspired his best-known work, *Peter Pan*. Highmore plays Peter Llewelen Davies, the boy most affected by his father's death. Things only get worse for Peter when his mother (played by Kate Winslet) becomes seriously ill. But his evolving relationship with Barrie helps him deal with his deep sorrow.

In a typical rave review, Todd McCarthy of *Variety* wrote: "Highmore is crucially emotive and heartrending as the boy whose name Barrie took for his fictional creation." His performance is "defiantly uncute," wrote Jonathan Dee in the *New York Times*. He noted that it is Highmore's "guardedness,

A scene from Charlie and the Chocolate Factory, *with Johnny Depp.*

that instinct not to show us everything so rare in a child actor that makes Highmore's performance so startlingly free of artifice." According to *Back Stage*, "As excellent as his costars Johnny Depp and Kate Winslet are in *Finding Neverland*, Highmore steals the film."

The film's director, Marc Forster, chose to shoot one of Highmore's key scenes early in the filming. He wanted both Johnny Depp and Kate Winslet to see the caliber of young actor with whom they would be working. Forster chose a scene in which Peter becomes enraged, tears up a book, and destroys a playhouse. "I wanted [them] to be aware that this is the tone and level of acting I expected from everyone and that [Highmore] was the standard, because there was not a false moment in this little kid," Forster said. After the scene, according to Forster, "Johnny just looked at me and said: 'Oh my God, this gift is scary.'" Winslet later confirmed Depp's impression, declaring that Highmore "is the most breathtaking child actor I have ever worked with, seen, or experienced in my life."

One of the hardest days of filming for Highmore was a crucial funeral scene. The challenge did not stem from the emotional intensity that the scene demanded, but rather from the fact that the scene was filmed beneath the busy flight path of a London airport. "[Every] half-minute we'd have to stop and wait for the planes," he recalled. The sickly appearance of his on-screen mother proved to be another distraction in several scenes. "When Kate [Winslet] didn't look well because of the makeup, we were all so worried," Highmore recalled. "We kept asking and checking to make sure she was OK. She had to keep telling us she was fine, it was only makeup."

Although his character was based on a real-life boy, Highmore did no research to prepare for the role. Instead, he read and re-read the script. "He's a very sad child," he said of Peter. "He's always thinking about his father. His father, even though he's dead, is still the most important person in Peter's life. And when Barrie tries to take over that role, Peter doesn't like it, so he tries to force him out." Getting into Peter's troubled mind was "quite easy," Highmore explained. "When you think about it, your dad's dead and your mum's dying, so, yes, it is quite sad."

Developing a Friendship with Johnny Depp

Despite the seriousness of his character, Highmore had a great time on the film set. He played football with his on-screen brothers, for example. Depp also helped him and the other young actors to keep loose. In one scene, for example, the children were expected to engage in silly behavior that disrupts a stodgy dinner gathering. Depp assisted by installing a whoopee cushion beneath the table without telling anyone. As the cameras started to roll, he let it rip. "I just let loose on the thing," Depp said. "The boys went crazy. I mean, they lost their minds."

"I liked my character, Charlie," said Highmore. "On the outside, it doesn't look like he's got much. He's poor. He eats cabbage soup. But he's kind and he has a family who loves him. So actually, he's got quite a lot."

Depp and Highmore became fast friends as the filming progressed. Depp called him "an amazing kid. Beyond that, he's an amazing guy. Very pure. Very honest. Very normal. That's very refreshing." Highmore returned Depp's compliments. "He's fantastic. Every scene you do with him is a special scene," he said. Both said that the hardest part of *Finding Neverland* was saying good bye to each other at the end of filming.

The separation turned out to be brief, however, because Depp recommended Highmore for a starring role in *Charlie and the Chocolate Factory*, another film in which Depp had a lead role. "It's neat, because, in the film, Charlie has a dream to visit the chocolate factory, and it comes true," Highmore said. "My dream was to work with Johnny again, and it also came true."

Charlie and the Chocolate Factory

Charlie and the Chocolate Factory was a new film version of the popular children's novel by Roald Dahl. In 1971 Dahl's book was made into a musical movie, *Willy Wonka and the Chocolate Factory*. The movie became a cult classic, in large part due to the performance of Gene Wilder as Willy Wonka. For the remake, director Tim Burton wanted to create a film that would be truer to the darkly humorous spirit of the original story. It features a poor boy, Charlie Bucket, who wins a golden ticket to tour the mysterious chocolate empire of Willy Wonka. He makes his once-in-a-lifetime visit with four other gold-ticket winners who turn out to represent a checklist of obnoxious kid behavior: a glutton, a gum-chomper, a spoiled rich girl, and a boy addicted to all things video. Highmore was cast to play humble, polite Charlie opposite Depp's Willy Wonka.

As the film begins, Charlie lives in a ramshackle, drab dump with his four bedridden grandparents and his downtrodden but loving parents. "I liked my character, Charlie. On the outside, it doesn't look like he's got much," Highmore said. "He's poor. He eats cabbage soup. But he's kind and he has a family who loves him. So actually, he's got quite a lot."

——— " ———

"I'm not sure what I'd like to do when I'm older," Highmore said. "I'm still quite young. I don't think I have to decide quite yet."

——— " ———

When Charlie enters Willie Wonka's factory, he finds a glistening candy wonderland. "Tim actually built the entire chocolate factory, from the grass on the ground to the real trees where the Oompa Loompas hide," Highmore marveled. It wasn't hard for him and the four other children to "act" awed and delighted. "All Tim Burton had to do was shoot our real thoughts," he said.

Charlie and the Chocolate Factory was generally a hit with audiences. But many critics gave it mixed reviews. A number of them questioned Johnny Depp's unusual portrayal of Wonka as a bobbed-haired, high-voiced character who was openly rude to the children. Todd McCarthy voiced a typical reaction in *Variety* when he described Depp's performance as ranging from "bizarrely riveting to one-note and vaguely creepy."

Nevertheless, many reviewers agreed with McCarthy that, in spite of its flaws, the film was inventive and well made. They reserved special praise for the performances given by Highmore and the other supporting players. *New Yorker* reviewer Anthony Lane noted that *Charlie and the Chocolate Factory* author Roald Dahl knew how to tap into the wishes and fears of the young. "[That] is why Freddie Highmore, as Charlie, is the nerve center of the film," Lane wrote. "[Highmore] is up for high jinks, but he sees through low tricks. You catch a straightforwardness in him, a sanity in his gaze, that Dahl would have trusted."

Charlie finds the golden ticket.

For Highmore, the film was a great experience, in part because of the presence of other children on the set. "It's great because other kids are around. Sometimes you can feel a bit lonely, you know, when you're just on your own, when you're the only kid," he said. "I've just been very lucky to have been able to have the chance [to play Charlie]. I'm similar to Charlie, I guess, in that way. He's been very lucky to have been able to go to the factory."

The filming also deepened Highmore's friendship with Depp, with whom he stays in touch by e-mail. "He's fantastic," Highmore said. "I also say chocolate's fantastic, but I think Johnny's better than chocolate, so I need another word for Johnny. Something better than fantastic."

Looking to the Future

Highmore seems poised for even greater screen success in the years to come. He is set to appear with Russell Crowe in *A Good Year*, which is scheduled to be released in 2006. He also will star as Arthur in *Arthur and the Minimoys*, based on the book by Luc Besson. The film will blend animation with live action. "Minimoys are small people about the size of a tooth," explained Highmore. "There's a treasure in the garden and they help me find it." He is also taking a leading role in *Awful End*, a film based on the children's book trilogy by Philip Ardagh.

Despite his acting success, though, Highmore refuses to commit to a life-long career in acting. "I'm not sure what I'd like to do when I'm older," he said. "I might want to travel and see the world. That would be quite fun. . . . I'm still quite young. I don't think I have to decide quite yet."

HOME AND FAMILY

Highmore lives in north London with his parents and brother.

HOBBIES AND OTHER INTERESTS

Highmore likes music and plays clarinet and guitar. He is a huge fan of his local London soccer team, or "football" team, as the British call the sport. He loves to play football himself, too. He also likes computers. "I play video games," he said, "but not as much as Mike Teavee," the boy addicted to video games in *Charlie and the Chocolate Factory*.

SELECTED FILMS

Women Talking Dirty, 1999
Jack and the Beanstalk: The Real Story, 2001
I Saw You, 2002
Two Brothers, 2004
Five Children and It, 2004
Finding Neverland, 2004
Charlie and the Chocolate Factory, 2005

HONORS AND AWARDS

Best Young Actor (Critic's Choice Awards): 2004, for *Finding Neverland*; 2005, for *Charlie and the Chocolate Factory*
Best Supporting Actor (Broadcast Film Critics Award): 2005, for *Finding Neverland*

FURTHER READING

Periodicals

Backstage West, Jan. 6, 2005, p.12
Boys' Life, July 2005, p.7
Chicago Sun-Times, July 10, 2005, p.1
New York Times, Nov. 14, 2004, sec. 6, p.71

Time, Nov. 29, 2004, p.155
USA Today, Nov. 12, 2004, p.E3; July 13, 2005, p.D3

ADDRESS

Freddie Highmore
Artists Rights Group Ltd.
4 Great Portland Street
London W1W 8PA
England

WORLD WIDE WEB SITES

http://chocolatefactorymovie.warnerbros.com
http://www.miramax.com/findingneverland

Tim Howard 1979-
American Professional Soccer Player
Goalkeeper for England's Manchester United
Soccer Team

BIRTH

Tim Howard was born on March 6, 1979, in North Brunswick, New Jersey. Howard was the product of a mixed-race and mixed-nationality marriage: his father, Matthew Howard, is African-American, and his mother, Esther Howard, is a Hungarian-born white woman. Howard has one older brother, Chris.

YOUTH

Howard's early years were shaped by the divorce of his parents when he was three years old. He and his brother lived with their mother in a cramped apartment in North Brunswick, in a heavily industrialized part of northeastern New Jersey. "It was a one-bedroom apartment she made into a three-bedroom apartment," remembered Howard. "I don't know how she did it." His mother worked several jobs to help provide for the family. Though Howard's father, a long-distance truck driver, did not live with the family, he was a regular presence in the lives of his two sons.

The Howard boys developed a love of sports from an early age. Their father bought the boys a variety of sports equipment before they even learned to walk, and he watched closely to see which sports they gravitated toward.

From early on, Tim took to both soccer and basketball. He maintained these interests throughout his youth, and as he entered middle school and high school he began to stand out as an athlete. In high school, for example, Howard averaged 15 points a game in basketball. During his senior year, he helped lift his team all the way to the state finals.

Tim Mulqueen, who coached Howard as a youth and later as a professional, described his abilities as a 12-year-old player like this: "[Howard] was probably the best player on the field. He could do anything he wanted.... He was a natural."

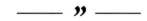

Where Howard really shined, however, was on the soccer field. He spent a lot of time in youth leagues as a midfielder, considered the most physically demanding of all the soccer positions. Midfielders have to be able to cover the entire field and demonstrate both offensive and defensive skills. But over time, he showed even more potential as a goalkeeper. By the time he reached middle school, his coaches were actively encouraging him to attend soccer camps to improve his goalkeeping skills. One coach who attested to his early skill was Tim Mulqueen, who coached Howard as a youth and later as a professional. Mulqueen later said that as a 12-year-old, "[Howard] was probably the best player on the field. He could do anything he wanted. . . . He was a natural." At age 15, he was selected to play in goal for a U.S. national team in tournaments against teams from other countries. He played on a U-17 team, a team consisting of players under the age of 17.

Diagnosed with Tourette's Syndrome

Howard's athletic skill helped him cope with a major challenge that he faced during his childhood. When Howard was around ten years old, he and his parents began to notice that he was developing strange mannerisms. He cleared his throat repeatedly and compulsively; he felt the need to touch objects in a specific order before he could move on to a different task; he recited certain numbers; and before he could talk to his mother, he felt a nearly uncontrollable impulse to touch her on the shoulders in a certain pattern.

As Howard's family struggled to understand what was happening, the youngster also felt embarrassed by his growing inability to conceal his odd habits from his schoolmates. "In the beginning, I wasn't very bothered about [TS] myself. I was just a kid, having fun, playing sports," Howard explained. But as he entered middle school and high school and became interested in girls, it became a bigger problem. "It hurt, especially coming into adolescence and high school," he continued. He knew that some classmates made fun of him behind his back, yet he never let the syndrome keep him from having a good high school experience. "Thankfully," he joked, "I was a popular guy—and I was big."

> "
>
> *"In the beginning, I wasn't very bothered about [Tourette's Syndrome] myself. I was just a kid, having fun, playing sports," Howard explained.*
>
> "

Around 1990, the mystery surrounding Howard's behavioral ticks was solved. He was diagnosed with a mild case of Tourette's Syndrome, a neurological disorder that is characterized by involuntary physical movements and vocal expressions. In its most severe forms, Tourette's Syndrome (or TS) causes some sufferers to involuntarily blurt out obscene words. This form of TS is called coprolalia. It is the source of most public misunderstandings of the disorder, since numerous television shows and movies have used this type of TS as a source of humor. Fortunately for Howard and his family, his case of TS was relatively mild.

EDUCATION

Howard attended public schools in North Brunswick, New Jersey. As he neared completion of his education at North Brunswick High School, Howard weighted whether to go on to college on an athletic scholarship or become a professional soccer player. College offered the opportunity to get an education and gain experience as a soccer player, but Howard knew that the opportunities to develop his soccer skills would be greater in the pro ranks.

Howard agonized about this choice until a month before his high school graduation. At that time he received an invitation from his old mentor Tim

Mulqueen that he decided he could not turn down. Mulqueen had become the coach for the North Jersey Imperials, a professional team in the Premier Development Soccer League (PDSL). This league was part of the MLS Project 40 program developed by Major League Soccer (MLS), the top professional soccer league in the United States. This program gave top young players a chance to learn from top soccer pros by including them on the rosters of various MLS teams.

Howard jumped at Mulqueen's invitation, and before he knew it he was training as a backup goalkeeper for the New Jersey MetroStars of the MLS. "I thought I would have taken a step back athletically [by going to college]," he explained. By the time he graduated from North Brunswick High School in 1997, he was already earning a paycheck from the PDSL.

CAREER HIGHLIGHTS

Learning with the Imperials

After joining the Imperials in 1997, Howard impressed his coaches with his confidence and athleticism. At 6' 3" and 210 pounds he was an imposing physical presence, with quick reflexes and strong hands. He was an aggressive keeper, moving forward to close off scoring attempts, yet he also played under control. Mulqueen acknowledged that Howard, like most young goalkeepers, needed to improve his decision making on the field. But he praised the netminder as someone who "never gets rattled. He's very composed."

Howard's maturity served him well during his second year in the pros. During the 1998 season, the MetroStars' starting goalkeeper, Tony Meola–who had led the U.S. squad in the 1994 World Cup—was benched after receiving a yellow-card suspension. Howard suddenly found himself slated as the team's starting goalkeeper for its next game, an August 18 tilt against the Colorado Rapids. He was nervous and flustered at the outset of the game, but he soon settled down and helped his team register a 4-1 victory. This triumph put the 19-year-old Howard in the MLS record book as the youngest goalkeeper ever to post a win in league history.

Balancing Pro and International Competition

During his first few years with the MetroStars Howard served as the backup keeper, first to Meola, then to Mike Ammann. During this apprenticeship Howard had the opportunity to represent his country in several international games and tournaments. He played on the U.S. U-20 (under 20) national squad, which made a strong showing in the 1999 World Youth Championship. Later that same year he got three starts (and allowed just two goals) for the U.S. U-23 (under 23) team at the Pan American Games. His strong performance helped the squad earn a bronze medal in that competi-

Howard played for five seasons with the MetroStars.

tion. In 2000 Howard served as a backup to goalkeeper Brad Friedel in the Summer Olympics, in which the U.S. team finished fourth.

Howard then returned to the MetroStars, where he trained furiously for an opportunity to be the team's starting goalkeeper. He got that chance at the start of the 2001 season, after Ammann was traded. Howard expressed excitement about the upcoming season, but he also knew that it would be a big challenge. He was still young for a goalkeeper, a position that often takes years to learn. Many top keepers don't reach their best form until they are in their early thirties. "It is somewhat unprecedented for a 21-year-old goal-keeper to get the full-time nod," he acknowledged.

As it turned out, Howard sparkled in his first season as a full-time starter. He played every minute of all 26 games played by the MetroStars, and although the team had only a marginally successful record of 13 wins, 10 losses, and 3 ties, he won accolades for his performance in goal. He allowed an average of just 1.33 goals per game, recorded 4 shutouts, and led the league with 146 saves. By the end of the season Howard had collected a stunning string of awards: he was named to the MLS All-Star Team and honored as MLS Goalkeeper of the Year, among several other awards.

The year 2001 was a milestone for Howard in another way as well, for it was the year that he acknowledged publicly that he had Tourette's Syndrome. Previously, he had worked hard to keep his symptoms in check, but he finally decided it was time to divulge his secret. He was pleasantly surprised to find that both his teammates and the press were quite supportive.

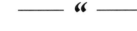

"[Tourette's Syndrome is] a hurdle, but it's certainly not a brick wall," said Howard. "A speed bump, but not a stop sign."

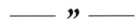

Before the year was out Howard had agreed to become a spokesman for the Tourette's Syndrome Association of New Jersey, a sure sign that he was growing more comfortable with talking about his illness. It also indicated his growing awareness that he could be a role model for others who suffered from TS. In fact, he made a point of talking to young people with TS and emphasizing that "[Tourette's Syndrome is] a hurdle, but it's certainly not a brick wall. A speed bump, but not a stop sign." MLS acknowledged Howard's community work by naming him the league's Humanitarian of the Year in 2001.

Stardom Brings Opportunity

Howard's second year as the starting keeper for the MetroStars was a bit of a disappointment, both for himself and his team. After finishing second in their division in 2001 the MetroStars fell to fourth in 2002. Howard's goals-against average rose to 1.66 per game, placing him tenth among goalkeepers in the league. Observers felt that the falloff was not due to his play, however. The MetroStars defense was weak throughout the season, and Howard faced more shots and made more saves than anyone in the league. In fact, his efforts earned him a spot on the MLS All-Star Team for a second straight year.

Howard's steady play with the MetroStars caught the attention of Tony Coton, who coached goalkeepers for Manchester United, a team in the English Pre-

In 2003 Howard joined Manchester United, the most famous soccer team in the world.

mier League (EPL). Manchester United is considered by many to be the most famous and perhaps the best professional soccer team in the world. Midway through the 2003 season, Coton and team manager Sir Alex Ferguson cut a deal with the MetroStars to bring Howard to Manchester United (often known by the nicknames Man United or just Man U).

Though he had been enjoying a terrific season with the first-place MetroStars, Howard was delighted to make the leap from the American league to the glamorous EPL. His salary soared from less than $30,000 a year to $1.4 million a year, with the promise of a $1.5-million bonus if he became the team's starting keeper. To the surprise of soccer fans across Europe, Howard was made starting keeper for Manchester United in an exhibition game played against Italian team Juventus at Giants Stadium in New Jersey. Just days after his mid-July acquisition, he shone in goal, leading Man United to a 4-1 victory.

Life with Man United

Though he wowed Man United coaches and American fans during the summer exhibition season, fans and the press in England were not so eager to embrace the young American keeper. Some of the English newspapers, in fact, were downright vicious. They referred to Howard as "disabled" and described him as "United's Zombie" because of his TS. The "zombie" reference reflected a belief that he took medication to control his Tourette's Syndrome; in reality, though, he has never taken any drugs to treat his TS because of concerns that the medication might dull his reflexes. But Howard shrugged off all the cruel remarks. "All sorts of dumb, silly things were written about me," he admitted. "I was not bothered. It could have impeded my career if I'd listened to the tabloids. But I don't read my own press, good or bad. I was quite comfortable with who I am and left it at that."

Instead, Howard focused on his soccer. He leapfrogged over famed French goalkeeper Fabien Barthez to win the opening-day start for Man United, then recorded a shutout as his team romped to a 4-0 victory. His run continued from there, as Howard became the regular starting keeper. He recorded 14 shutouts for the 2003-04 season, and Man United lost just three of its first 20 games. Howard suddenly found himself a celebrity in football-mad Manchester, unable to walk down the street or go out to a movie without being recognized and hounded by autograph seekers. As in the United States, fans embraced the handsome, soft-spoken American keeper and set aside their concerns that his Tourette's Syndrome might somehow cost their team a match. Even the notoriously hostile English press warmed to him. "He has the aura of a brick wall," declared the *Daily Telegraph*. "A lot of goalkeepers want to look good . . . [but Howard] doesn't mind making ugly saves. It's the sign of a great goalkeeper."

Howard's honeymoon ended in March 2004, when a brief stretch of inconsistent play led Ferguson to bench him in favor of backup keeper Roy Carroll. Instead of complaining about being benched, Howard praised Ferguson for recognizing that he needed a break and set his sights on regaining his competitive edge. He returned to goal in late April, in time to close out the remaining games of the EPL season. He then prepared to face Milwall in the FA Cup, an annual competition between the top professional teams in England. Howard was spectacular in helping Manchester United cruise to a 3-0 victory. This triumph made him the first American player to play for a team winning the FA Cup.

"All sorts of dumb, silly things were written about me," Howard admitted. "I was not bothered. It could have impeded my career if I'd listened to the tabloids. But I don't read my own press, good or bad. I was quite comfortable with who I am and left it at that."

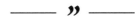

Reflecting on his strong finish to the 2003-04 season, Howard stated that he was "certainly a much better goalkeeper now than when I came to the club. Before, I was more of an athlete wearing goalkeeper gloves. But in my time here . . . I've become more than just an athlete; I feel I've become a goalkeeper." Premier League players agreed, naming him Keeper of the Year.

Struggles Lead to Demotion

Howard began Man United's 2004-05 campaign as the number one keeper, but early mistakes diminished Ferguson's confidence in his young player and he was soon demoted to second string behind Roy Carroll. Over the course of the year Howard played in some 30 games, but he never displayed the consistency that he had shown in his first year.

Howard in goal for Manchester United, 2004.

At season's end, Manchester management shuffled its goalkeeping corps with a series of moves that sent mixed signals about Howard's future. On the one hand, he was signed to a lucrative four-year contract that would keep him with the team through 2009. But the team also signed Dutch goal-keeping sensation Edwin Van Der Sar to a two-year contract and named him their number one keeper. The Man United coaches explained that in Van Der Sar, they had signed not only the best goalkeeper of the present, but someone who could serve as a mentor to Howard, who they still saw as the team's goalkeeper of the future.

British fans and newspapers speculated that Howard was unhappy about taking a back seat to Van Der Sar, but he denied these reports. "It's not easy in Europe," he said, "and it never was going to be easy. Do I just pack up and leave and go somewhere where it's easier? I could, a lot of people would and do. I chose not to do that. I choose to fight it out."

As the 2005-06 season kicked off, Howard found himself in the familiar if somewhat frustrating position of being a back-up goal keeper for both Man-chester United and the United States national team. By 21 games into Man United's 2005-06 season, Howard had been given the starting nod only three times. Meanwhile, head coach Bruce Arena of the U.S. national team contin-ued to refer to Howard as the "keeper of the future." Many viewed this as a sign that veterans Kasey Keller or Brad Friedel are more likely to be the starting netminder for the Americans in the 2006 World Cup, the world championship of international soccer.

Nonetheless, many soccer analysts believe that Howard is destined for greater stardom in the future. They point out that he is only now reaching the age at which most goalkeepers are considered to reach their prime. And they note that he has already proven himself as a legitimate goalkeeper in the most competitive league in Europe. For his part, Howard has expressed continued determination to be recognized someday as one of the best goalkeepers in the world.

MARRIAGE AND FAMILY

Howard became engaged to his wife, Laura, early in 2003. The couple planned to be married in the fall of that year in a big wedding. Howard's July 2003 signing with England's Manchester United disrupted those plans, however. Eager to move to England together, the couple arranged a hasty marriage ceremony in New York's Central Park with a handful of friends and family. They had their first child late in 2005.

The Howards live most of the year in a country house outside of Manchester, England, but they also keep a home in Germantown, Tennessee, a suburb of Laura's hometown of Memphis.

HOBBIES AND OTHER INTERESTS

A quiet man of strong Christian faith, Howard does not drive fancy cars or spend money on expensive hobbies. He enjoys spending the offseason in Tennessee, where he is not hounded by soccer fans as he is in England. "[I like doing] all the stuff I can't do in England," he said. "Just hanging out, enjoying time with my family."

HONORS AND AWARDS

Major League Soccer (MLS) Keeper of the Year: 2001
Major League Soccer (MLS) Humanitarian of the Year: 2001
Major League Soccer (MLS) All-Star: 2001, 2002
English Premier League Keeper of the Year (Professional Footballers Association): 2004

FURTHER READING

Periodicals

Current Biography Yearbook, 2005
Daily Telegraph (London), May 13, 2005, p.17
Esquire, June 2004, p.70

Manchester Evening News, Sep. 9, 2003, p. SPT8; May 21, 2004, p.SPT2; Apr. 5, 2005, p.SPT2
Observer (London), Aug. 1, 2004, p.61
Philadelphia Inquirer, July 26, 2004, p.D1
Soccer Digest, Dec. 2002, p.36
Sports Illustrated, Aug. 11, 2003, p.60; Mar. 22, 2004, p.90
USA Today, July 31, 2003, p.C11; Jan. 23, 2004, p.A1

Online Articles

http://www.ussoccer.com/bio/index.jsp_1728.html
(*U.S. Soccer*, "Biographies: Tim Howard," undated)

Online Databases

Biography Resource Center Online, 2004

ADDRESS

Tim Howard
Manchester United
Sir Matt Busby Way
Manchester M16 0RA
England

WORLD WIDE WEB SITES

http://www.manutd.com
http://www.tsa-usa.org

Rachel McAdams 1976-

Canadian Actress
Star of the Hit Movies *Mean Girls*, *The Notebook*,
Wedding Crashers, and *Red Eye*

BIRTH

Rachel McAdams was born in London, Ontario, Canada, on
October 7, 1976. Her mother, Sandra, is a nurse. Her father,
Lance, is a truck driver. She has a younger brother, Daniel, and
a younger sister, Kayleen.

YOUTH

McAdams, who describes herself as a "little hick girl from Canada," grew up in the small town of St. Thomas, near London.

She loved to perform from an early age and staged productions in the back-yard with her sister as her "trusty sidekick." At age seven she told her parents she wanted to be a performer. "[They] didn't discourage me, but they didn't go out and find me an agent," she said.

Naturally athletic, McAdams figure skated competitively from about age four through high school. But she found solo skating "a fairly ruthless sport in terms of time and energy." When she teamed up with a synchronized skating group, things lightened up a little. "We wore costumes and blue eye shadow up to our eyebrows and a bottle of hair spray each," she remembered with a laugh.

———— " ————

"I'd always wanted to do musicals, so I signed up for the Disney camp, and I was so embarrassed," McAdams recalled. "I was with these eight-year-olds who were going to be Broadway stars, singing at the top of their lungs, dancing since they were two. I was so clumsy, I would just go home and cry."

———— " ————

McAdams found a more satisfying outlet for her performing desires in the theater camps that she attended from about age 12. She admits, though, that her first experiences at the camp were discouraging. "I'd always wanted to do musicals, so I signed up for the Disney camp, and I was so embarrassed," she recalled. "I was with these eight-year-olds who were going to be Broadway stars, singing at the top of their lungs, dancing since they were two. I was so clumsy, I would just go home and cry."

Luckily, she was steered to drama via the plays of William Shakespeare, the renowned 16th-century English playwright. "The [camp] director came up to me and said, 'Maybe you'd be happier in the Shakespeare group.'" McAdams said. "I said, 'I can't do Shakespeare.' So he says, 'Well, you can't sing or dance, either!'"

Despite her reservations, McAdams immediately fell in love with acting. "I did Shakespeare in this outdoor Greek amphitheater at 12 years old," she recalled. "We were playing fairies in *A Midsummer Night's Dream*. We wore our beach towels as capes, and our director would play [music by Irish singer] Enya. He'd turn on this beautiful music, it was nine in the morning, and I just remember peering out through my beach-towel cape, seeing incredible trees and the sun coming through, and thinking, 'All right, I can see doing this for a while.'"

Over the next few years McAdams worked hard at developing her acting abilities. Audiences soon took notice. In 1995, for example, she won a prestigious acting prize when her high school group performed at a regional drama festival. "For Rachel to get that award tells how even in her high school years she stood out," said Linda Maskell Pereira, her drama teacher, who co-directed the play. "This was an ensemble, and the lines were evenly distributed between 22 people. But Rachel held your attention."

EDUCATION

McAdams attended her local high school in St. Thomas, where she was a far cry from the teen queen she portrayed in the film *Mean Girls*. "High school was hard," she said. "I didn't have a group. I had me." She admitted that her insecurity sometimes drove her to be less than kind to her fellow students. The few times someone would invite her into a group, the talk often was negative and critical of others. "That I feel bad for," she said. "But it came out of this place of just wanting to belong, and I think that's so much of what gossip is. If you're the follower, you usually just want that sort of approval."

"*[Gossiping in high school] came out of this place of just wanting to belong, and I think that's so much of what gossip is,*" McAdams said. "*If you're the follower, you usually just want that sort of approval.*"

Even in her last year of high school, social pressures remained strong for McAdams. As a senior, she joined the student council simply to make use of the council's private office at lunchtime. She was relieved to be able to avoid the lunchroom, where "you'd never sit at a table where you didn't belong, so that dreaded walk through the cafeteria was like a death march."

As her high school graduation approached, McAdams planned to major in cultural studies at York University in Toronto. But a last-minute intervention by her drama teacher, Maskell Pereira, steered her toward acting. "She literally grabbed me the day before university applications were due and said, 'Why aren't you going into theater?'" McAdams recalled. "It just ignited something that had been there and that I hadn't been brave enough to follow through with." McAdams immediately changed her application to theater studies.

When McAdams started college, one of her instructors, David Rotenberg, remembered that "she was shy, but sort of had a twinkle. By the time she got to me in the fourth year, she was landed, she had feet." His confidence in her abilities led him to cast her as the lead in the play *Lulu* by Frank

Wedekind. "It was fascinating to watch the agents watch her, their eyes rolling back into their heads [during her performance]," he remembered. "They came chasing me after the first act." McAdams earned a bachelor of fine arts (BFA) degree in theater studies at York in the late 1990s.

FIRST JOBS

McAdams nabbed her first paid professional acting jobs when she was still at York. She took small roles on a number of television programs, and during spring break of her senior year, she signed on for her first feature film. In this film, an Italian-Canadian production called *My Name Is Tanino*, McAdams played a wealthy American girl on a European vacation who is romanced by an Italian film student named Tanino. The action revolves around the film student's misadventures when he comes to the United States to pursue her. Though little noticed, the 2002 film did give McAdams the opportunity to ride an airplane for the first time. "When the [flight attendants] were offering the newspaper, I was like, 'Do I have to pay you?' I just had no idea how anything worked," she recalled.

> In her high school lunchroom, "you'd never sit at a table where you didn't belong, so that dreaded walk through the cafeteria was like a death march."

McAdams's next role was as a 15-year-old in the Canadian independent film, *Perfect Pie*, released in 2002. The role won her national recognition, including a nomination for a Genie Award, the Canadian equivalent of an Oscar. In spite of her success, McAdams still did not see herself as bound for Hollywood, the center of the American film industry. "I thought I would refuse to be part of it," she said. "I thought, 'I'm just going to do theater and be poor, and it will be really romantic.'"

But by this time McAdams had already taken her first cautious steps toward Hollywood. In 2001 she auditioned for a pilot television show based on the Nancy Drew mystery novels. "I didn't get it, and I was devastated," she said. "I thought I'd blown my only chance." Feeling she had nothing to lose, she tried out for a role in *The Hot Chick*, a comedy starring the comedian Rob Schneider. To her complete amazement, she got the part.

The Hot Chick

In *The Hot Chick* (2002), McAdams plays the title role of a gorgeous high-school cheerleader with a nasty streak. When a small-time crook, played by

Schneider, steals her magical earrings, the two change personalities and physiques. The movie exploits the crude humorous possibilities that might occur if a self-absorbed teenage blonde woke up as a nerdy 30-year-old man and he woke up in a young female body. Critics generally panned the film, but acknowledged that fans of raunchy humor would love it. "*The Hot Chick* is completely ridiculous, and involves toe-curling scenes of gender confusion and inappropriate sexual advances," declared the *Toronto Sun* in a typical review. "All the more reason for the target audience to love this film."

McAdams didn't attract much attention playing second fiddle to Schneider. "[The role was] such a strange little entrance to make," she said. "I guess it could have been an exit as well." But McAdams continued to work. She returned to Canada to act in a television miniseries called "Slings and Arrows." She played the role of an actress from small-town Ontario who wins the role of Ophelia in the Shakespeare play *Hamlet*, then pursues the actor who plays the title role. Her performance won McAdams a Genie Award for best actress in 2003.

"Regina is absolutely in a league of her own at the very top," McAdams confided about her character in **Mean Girls**. *"She and her friends practically run the school, since they dictate what's cool and what's not, the style of clothing everyone should wear, and how people should behave."*

Mean Girls

McAdams then returned to the United States to take a leading role in *Mean Girls* (2004), a comedy set in a suburban high school. The movie stars Lindsay Lohan as Cady, a girl entering an American high school after years of being home-schooled in Africa by her anthropologist parents. Cady quickly discovers that, when it comes to the struggle for social survival, teenagers are more vicious than beasts. At the top of her school's food chain is Regina George—played by McAdams—the attractive but thoroughly nasty leader of the Plastics, a clique of shallow, popular girls. "Regina is absolutely in a league of her own at the very top," McAdams confirmed. "She and her friends practically run the school, since they dictate what's cool and what's not, the style of clothing everyone should wear, and how people should behave."

The director of *Mean Girls*, Mark S. Waters, helped McAdams tap into mean-girl instincts by giving her tapes of classic screen villains like Joan Crawford. Her best inspiration, though, turned out to be Alec Baldwin's ruthless character in the movie *Glengarry Glen Ross*. Equally rousing was the punk rock band Hole. "I was jogging and listening to [Hole lead singer]

McAdams (second from right) took Hollywood by storm as the conniving teen queen Regina in Mean Girls. *Fellow "mean girls" in the film included Lindsay Lohan (left) as Cady, Amanda Seyfried (second from left) as Karen, and Lacey Chabert (right) as Gretchen.*

Courtney Love and getting totally revved up," McAdams said. "It makes you feel angry somehow, but empowered and filled with this weird, carnal strength."

Critics and audiences loved *Mean Girls*, describing it as a definite cut above the usual teen-flick storyline. "In a wasteland of dumb movies about teenagers, *Mean Girls* is a smart and funny one," wrote reviewer Roger Ebert in the *Chicago Sun-Times*. "It even contains some wisdom." McAdams, meanwhile, won special praise for her portrayal of outrageously self-centered Regina. "[McAdams is] the funniest of the Plastics," according to *USA Today*. "[She uses] both her blond looks and comic flair to make a direct hit as a high school villainess."

The Notebook

If *Mean Girls* was a showcase for McAdams's comic sparkle, her next release, *The Notebook* (2004), revealed her dramatic depth. Based on a best-selling novel by Nicholas Sparks, the film depicts passionate lovers separated by class prejudice. McAdams plays the role of Allie, a feisty southern debutante. She falls in love with Duke (played by Ryan Gosling), a boy from the sawmill who is as unsuitable as he is irresistible. Their story is told as a series of flashbacks from the present day, as an elderly man reads chapters from a notebook to his ailing wife. "When I read the script I couldn't stop crying," she said. "It's a big, sweeping, epic love story and the biggest lead I've ever done. I'm a hopeless romantic; I'm a softie and smooshy inside. It's a very honest and pure love story and they are not told as much as they should be."

McAdams tried out for the role of Allie after it was turned down by established star Reese Witherspoon. The director, Nick Cassavettes, said that a dozen better-known and more experienced performers also were under consideration. But McAdams gave a terrific audition, and she got the part. Gosling declared that her natural spirit and empathy set her apart from the other actresses. "We needed somebody who was going to step in and say, 'I'm a girl. I know [how to play Allie]. Shut up and roll the camera,'" he said. "We needed that because the character was such a strong character. The truth is, I don't think we would have done the movie without Rachel. This is Rachel's movie. She's driving it."

> "When I read the script [for **The Notebook**] I couldn't stop crying," McAdams said. "It's a big, sweeping, epic love story and the biggest lead I've ever done. I'm a hopeless romantic; I'm a softie and smooshy inside. It's a very honest and pure love story and they are not told as much as they should be."

To help transform a small-town Ontario girl to a wealthy Southern belle, Cassavettes enrolled McAdams in etiquette classes and ballet lessons. She also attended several fancy weddings in the American South and talked with debutantes. But she created most of the character of Allie straight from her heart. "I just saw someone [who] was just really hungry for life and life experience and for love, someone who was really brave, and I have that in my life," McAdams explained. "I tend to attack things head on. I wouldn't be out here coming from a small town unless I sort of had that sense."

By coincidence, Gosling grew up in London, Ontario, only a few miles from where McAdams was raised. They even discovered they had been born in the same hospital. But the two had never met before filming. This factor, combined with the intimate nature of the movie, made it a challenge for the two actors to develop the necessary comfort level with each other. "There are so many trust issues and you're working all that stuff out in the begin-

*The on-screen kiss between McAdams and co-star
Ryan Gosling was a big hit with movie fans.*

ning," McAdams explained. "It takes a lot of time." By the end of filming, though, their chemistry was clearly convincing: The two picked up several fans' awards for their on-screen romance, and when McAdams and Gosling accepted an MTV Movie Award for best on-screen smooch of 2005, they replayed their passionate kiss at the podium.

Some critics complained that *The Notebook* was too sweet and syrupy to be considered a top-notch film. But many reviewers noted that the performances turned in by McAdams and her co-stars lifted the movie above the level of a typical tear-jerker. "McAdams's expressive beauty moved thrillingly between rapture and heartbreak," noted the *Los Angeles Times* reviewer. A *Detroit News* critic heralded her as a "full-blown dramatic actress who has to deal with tragedy, conflict, and heartache, all while winning over the audience."

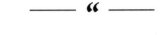

As for McAdams, she was happy for the opportunity to move on froom her comic teen-aged roles. "It was a drastic change, but it certainly was a welcome change," she said. "I always imagined myself doing drama instead of comedy." She said it would be hard to ever return to younger roles. "*The Notebook* changed me. I grew up a little bit, and I don't think I can go back," she said. "*Mean Girls* was kind of my last hurrah playing a 16-year-old. I'm ready to move on."

McAdams said that Wilson always kept her on her toes while shooting **Wedding Crashers**. *"He'd always do something silly right before the cameras rolled," she said. "He'd make funny faces or whisper something."*

Wedding Crashers

McAdams returned to comedy for her next role, in the 2005 hit comedy *Wedding Crashers*. The film stars Owen Wilson and Vince Vaughan as zany lawyers who crash wedding receptions to pick up women. McAdams plays a supporting role in the film as a bridesmaid at a wedding that they crash. When Wilson falls in love with her, it causes a rift between the buddies. McAdams said that Wilson always kept her on her toes during shooting. "He'd always do something silly right before the cameras rolled," she said. "He'd make funny faces or whisper something."

McAdams called both Wilson and Vaughan "comic geniuses." But the actor she most connected with on the shoot was Christopher Walken, who played her father. "One of the last scenes I shot was with him. We were in the flower

Claire (McAdams) and John (Owen Wilson) in a scene from Wedding Crashers.

market, and I don't know, there was this synergy," she said. The movie and her performance were generally well reviewed. A reviewer for *Maclean's* magazine singled out "a star-making performance by McAdams, who has the most radiant smile since Audrey Hepburn."

Indeed, with this role McAdams really began to stand out to critics—even though she played a secondary role in the film. "It's not easy to pigeonhole actress Rachel McAdams," wrote reviewer Marcy Medina. "There are her ever-changing hairdos, for one—from the long platinum tresses in *Mean Girls* to the flame-colored waves in *The Notebook* to the brown curls in her most recent film, *Wedding Crashers*. And so far, each character on her resume bears little resemblance to the last. The one constant, however, is her engaging screen presence that keeps moviegoers' eyes on McAdams whenever she appears."

Red Eye

Soon after the release of *Wedding Crashers*, yet another McAdams film hit American movie theatres. In this movie, *Red Eye* (2005), she proved that she could knock out audiences in another movie genre: the thriller. *Red Eye* was directed by Wes Craven, creator of teen-slasher classics like *A Nightmare on Elm Street* and *Scream*. Unlike those notoriously bloody films, though, *Red Eye* relied on subtlety and escalating suspense to keep audiences riveted to their seats.

McAdams stars as Lisa Reisert, a hotel manager on her way home from her grandmother's funeral on a late-night flight. After a preflight encounter with Jackson Rippner, a handsome stranger, Reisert finds herself seated beside him on the plane. At first the two carry on a flirtatious dialogue, but once they are in the air he reveals that he is a terrorist plotting to kill a government official scheduled to stay at her hotel. He informs her that if she doesn't help him carry out the assassination, her father will be murdered by an accomplice. "It's a pretty dire situation," McAdams said. "If she helps Jackson carry out his plot, she is as much a murderer as he is."

Most of *Red Eye* takes place in the claustrophobic airplane cabin. "The psychological mind play between these two characters in that confined space was the element I was most attracted to in the script," McAdams said. "[Not] having a lot of dialogue, having to have a lot of the work done kind of behind your eyes and hoping that it comes across: The subtleties were so significant."

People magazine called *Red Eye* "the kind of solid mainstream film making that has become all too rare in recent years." The reviewer singled out McAdams for a rave review: "As the resourceful Reisert, McAdams, whose work has grown more confident with each film since last year's *Mean Girls*, blossoms into a movie star. With a face so expressive it could probably act out the alphabet, McAdams manages to outsmile Julia Roberts and outcry Demi Moore."

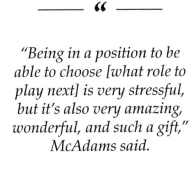

"Being in a position to be able to choose [what role to play next] is very stressful, but it's also very amazing, wonderful, and such a gift," McAdams said.

The Family Stone and Future Projects

McAdams returned to a supporting role for the holiday 2005 release, *The Family Stone*. Playing the youngest in a family of five, she joined an ensemble cast including Dermot Mulroney and Luke Wilson as her brothers, Sarah Jessica Parker as Mulroney's uptight girlfriend, and Diane Keaton and Craig Nelson as her parents. In this generally well-received "meet-the-parents" comedy, McAdams and Keaton scheme together to derail Mulroney's romance. The film earned mixed reviews, as some critics found the characters and plot twists not completely believable. But McAdams still earned praised for her work as sister Amy Stone, as in this review from *Vogue* magazine: "You may leave the theater talking about rising star Rachel McAdams, who shone in two of the summer's hits, *Wedding Crashers* and *Red Eye*. Well versed in playing teenage vixens—she was Lindsay Lohan's archenemy in *Mean Girls*—this 29-year-old Canadian makes Amy Stone an enjoyably wicked piece of work, a beauty whose venom is all the more lethal because she smiles so prettily."

Without a doubt, the positive "buzz" about McAdams that started with *Mean Girls* has grown with each successive role. Critics and colleagues agree that she is well on her way to major movie stardom. "She hates being compared, but I often said to her, 'You can be Meryl Streep. You can be Sigourney Weaver or Julia Roberts,'" said David Dobkin, director of *Wedding Crashers*. Wes Craven, director of *Red Eye*, called her a performer "of enormous range and great charisma . . . not to mention a fantastic beauty." In its end-of-year 2005 issue, *People* magazine designated Mc-Adams the year's "Rising Star."

> ———— **"** ————
>
> *"My life comes to a screeching halt when I'm not making movies. I really like to ride my bike around town, garden, cook, and play Ultimate Frisbee,"* McAdams said. *"It's better than going to the gym. It's really social, you're outside with other people....* *I'm hooked."*
>
> ———— **"** ————

McAdams admits that she sometimes feels bowled over by her sudden and dramatic rise to stardom. "It's exciting and daunting all at the same time," she said of her success. "And I'm hesitant and overwhelmed and overjoyed." McAdams is also excited about a number of future films she is considering, noting that "opportunities are definitely coming up.... Being in a position to be able to choose [what role to play next] is very stressful, but it's also very amazing, wonderful, and such a gift."

HOME AND FAMILY

McAdams owns a house in Toronto. The city is "my home," she said. "It suits who I am and it helps me step away from the business.... When I'm in Toronto I spend time with friends and family."

HOBBIES AND OTHER INTERESTS

"My life comes to a screeching halt when I'm not making movies," McAdams said. "I really like to ride my bike around town, garden, cook, and play Ultimate Frisbee," a combination of soccer and football with a flying disk. "It's better than going to the gym," she said. "It's really social, you're outside with other people.... I'm hooked."

When McAdams is in Toronto, she also likes to play pool and hang out at Stones Place, a bar that features memorabilia from the English rock group, the Rolling Stones. She is well known for her sweet tooth. "I always get in trouble for drinking my mom's maple syrup," she said.

In spite of her home-loving ways, McAdams has a sense of adventure, too. In recent years she has taken backpacking trips through parts of Australia and Costa Rica.

SELECTED FILM CREDITS

My Name Is Tanino, 2002
The Hot Chick, 2002
Mean Girls, 2004
The Notebook, 2004
Wedding Crashers, 2005
Red Eye, 2005
The Family Stone, 2005

HONORS AND AWARDS

Best Supporting Actress in a Drama Series (Genie Awards): 2003 for
    "Slings and Arrows"
Best On-Screen Team (MTV Movie Awards): 2005, with Lacey Chabert
    and Amanda Seyfried, for *Mean Girls*
Breakthrough Female (MTV Movie Awards): 2005, for *Mean Girls*
Best Movie Actress in a Drama (Teen Choice Awards): 2005,
    for *The Notebook*

FURTHER READING

Books

Who's Who in America, 2006

Periodicals

Allure, Nov. 1, 2005, p.189
Backstage West, Jan. 6, 2005, p.12
Boston Herald, June 20, 2004, p.A3
Chicago Tribune, Aug. 18, 2005, p.10; Aug. 20, 2005, p.C21
Entertainment Weekly, June 18, 2004, p.52
Interview, July 2005, p.54
Los Angeles Times, May 8, 2005
Newsweek, Aug. 22, 2005, p.77
Ottawa Citizen, May 22, 2004, p.L5
People, July 12, 2004, p.114
Toronto Star, July 11, 2004, p.D8
Toronto Sun, June 20, 2004, p.S18
USA Today, June 25, 2004, p.D3; July 7, 2004, p.2

Online Databases

Biography Resource Center Online, 2004

ADDRESS

Rachel McAdams
Gersh Agency
41 Madison Avenue
33rd Floor
New York, NY 10010

WORLD WIDE WEB SITES

http://www.meangirls.com
http://www.thenotebookmovie.com
http://www.redeye-themovie.com
http://www.weddingcrashersmovie.com
http://www.thefamilystone.com

Rosa Parks 1913-2005
American Civil Rights Activist
Recipient of the Congressional Gold Medal of Honor

AN ICON OF THE CIVIL RIGHTS MOVEMENT

Perhaps every American knows the name Rosa Parks. Throughout her life, she fought through peaceful means for the rights of all people. Parks became a hero to African Americans and civil rights activists around the United States when, during a time and in a place of intense racism and segregation, she refused to give up her seat on the bus to a white man. Her simple but courageous action led to a 381-day bus boycott in Montgomery, Alabama. The boycott brought an end to bus segregation in Montgomery—and, more importantly, it sparked the modern-day civil rights movement.

Rosa Parks died of natural causes at her home in Detroit, Michigan, on October 24, 2005. She was 92. For a week, the whole country celebrated her life and mourned her death. Three separate funerals were held in three different cities—Montgomery, Alabama; Washington, DC; and Detroit, Michigan. Thousands of mourners waited for hours at each location to say good-bye. Rosa and her late husband, Raymond Parks, did not have any children. She is survived by one aunt, 13 nieces and nephews, and numerous cousins. (For additional information on Parks, see also earlier profiles in *Biography Today*, 1992, and Update in 1994 Annual Cumulation.)

EARLY YEARS

Rosa Parks was born on February 4, 1913, in Tuskegee, Alabama. She grew up in a time when discrimination was a way of life for African Americans in the United States, particularly in the South. African Americans did not have the same rights as their white counterparts.

> *Parks recalled, "I never had more than five or six months of education a year while the white children went to school for nine months."*

Like most blacks in the South at the time, Parks grew up poor. Her father, James McCauley, was a carpenter. Her mother, Leona McCauley, was a schoolteacher. Rosa's parents separated when she was very young. After that, Rosa, her mother, and her younger brother, Sylvester, went to live with her grandparents in Pine Level, Alabama. Parks would often accompany her grandparents to pick crops on nearby plantations. It was not unusual for black children to work in the fields to earn money to help support their families. In fact, some black schools closed three months earlier than the schools for white children so that the black children could work in the fields. Parks recalled, "I never had more than five or six months of education a year while the white children went to school for nine months."

Parks grew up during a period of U.S. history in which black Americans did not have the same rights and opportunities that white Americans enjoyed. This was especially apparent in the country's southern states, where racist attitudes towards black people remained strong in many white communities. In fact, all of the southern states built political and social systems that were blatantly unfair to African-American citizens. For example, southern states like Alabama embraced the system of segregation, which kept white and black people separated from one another in most aspects of everyday life. Segregation was enforced in restaurants, theaters, buses, and other public places. This was based on an 1896 Supreme Court case, *Plessy v. Ferguson*, which created the concept of "separate but equal." In nearly every instance, though, the facilities that were designated for whites were much nicer and cleaner than those that were assigned to blacks. Alabama was one of several states that supported separate schools for white and black children. This was perhaps the most destructive element of segregation, since these schools provided an inferior education that further limited opportunities for African Americans.

Many African-American people resented the unequal system in which they lived. But black communities of the American South were powerless to change things. White men occupied nearly every important political and law enforcement office across the South, and most of them did not want African Americans to gain greater political, economic, or social power. As a result, they used a variety of means to keep black families "in their place." For example, some officials forced African Americans to pass difficult written tests before they would allow them to register to vote. The poll tax was another popular tool to repress the black vote, because most black people were so poor that they could not afford the expense. Finally, whites used violence and intimidation to make sure that African Americans remained in their inferior position in society.

—— " ——

"Back then, we didn't have any rights," Parks wrote in her autobiography. "It was just a matter of survival, ... of existing from one day to the next. I remember going to sleep as a girl and hearing the Klan ride at night and hearing a lynching and being afraid the house would burn down."

—— " ——

Parks was aware of the inequalities she faced as a black child growing up in the South. She saw how blacks worked in the fields for meager wages, lived in impoverished homes, ate in segregated restaurants, attended substandard schools, and even drank from separate drinking fountains. Even as a child, she knew this was wrong. Worse yet, she saw black men being harassed and beaten by white men simply because of the color of their skin and black churches being burned by the Ku Klux Klan. "Back then, we didn't have any rights," Parks wrote in her autobiography, *Rosa Parks: My Story.* "It was just a matter of survival, . . . of existing from one day to the next. I remember going to sleep as a girl and hearing the Klan ride at night and hearing a lynching and being afraid the house would burn down."

EDUCATION

Leona McCauley wanted the best for her daughter, and she particularly stressed the importance of education. When Parks was 11, her mother had

Parks was a seamstress in 1955, at the time of the Montgomery bus boycott.

saved up enough money to send her to the Montgomery Industrial School for Girls, a private school run by whites from the North. Parks lived with her aunt while attending the school, which was burned down twice by whites who were trying to close it. Rosa recalled the most important lesson she learned at school was "that I was a person with dignity and self-respect, and I should not set my sights lower than anybody else just because I was black." These sentiments reinforced what she learned from her family at home. Her grandfather kept a shotgun nearby in case any Klansmen bothered his family. He refused to call white men "Mr." and told Rosa and her brother that they should not put up with mistreatment. In her autobiography, Parks wrote, "It was passed down almost in our genes."

Parks later attended a high school run by the Alabama State Teachers College, but was forced to drop out at the age of 16 to care for her aging grandparents and her mother. She returned to high school after she was married and earned her high school diploma in 1933 at the age of 20.

TAKING PART IN THE CIVIL RIGHTS MOVEMENT

From a young age, Rosa was very involved in her church, the African Methodist Episcopal (AME) Church. Her strong faith continued throughout her life. She loved to sing and pray. In her teen years, she also started to get involved in some of the local civil rights organizations. When she was 19 years old, Rosa met a barber named Raymond Parks through a mutual friend. They both shared a passion for civil rights and found that they had much in common, including their love of God. The two married in December 1932. It was through his encouragement that she decided to return to school to earn her high school diploma.

Together, Rosa and Raymond worked to gain equal rights for all Americans. Raymond was a member of the National Committee to Save the Scottsboro Boys, an organization formed to support a group of nine young black men who had been falsely accused of raping a white woman in 1931. He and Rosa were both involved in the Montgomery Voters League, whose purpose was to encourage blacks to vote and to become politically empowered. Parks recalled that they had a difficult time getting blacks registered to vote. "Even if we succeeded in getting applications filled out," she said, "the registrars would take them and tell us we would hear from them by mail if we passed. Very few ever heard, of course. Whites got their certificates right away. If ever you did get registered, you had to pay poll tax."

One particular incident of racism had a deep effect on Rosa Parks. While riding on a bus, she saw a young black soldier step in front of the bus. The driver got off and beat the soldier with a metal ticket puncher until the soldier was so badly hurt that he had to go to the hospital. Parks attended the trial of the bus driver, who was fined $24 for assault and battery—but he didn't lose his job. That incident inspired her to join the Montgomery chapter of the National Association for the Advancement of Colored People (NAACP) in 1943; she was soon elected secretary. At the NAACP, she worked to set up meetings, arranged speakers, helped people to register to vote, and worked with youth groups. Parks became quite well known in the Montgomery area for her civil rights activities and was well respected by the black community. She also attended an interracial leadership workshop at the Highlander Folk School in Tennessee, which trained its students to work for civil rights. At this school, she studied side-by-side with blacks and whites from all over the country who were dedicated to fighting segregation.

THE MOMENT THAT CHANGED AMERICA

In 1955, Rosa Parks was working as a seamstress for the Montgomery Fair department store. At that time, the bus was the main source of transportation for most blacks in Montgomery, including Parks. She rode the bus to and from work. Even though as many as 75% of the bus passengers were black, it was the black passengers who were treated poorly. They were forced to sit in the back of the bus. If a white passenger boarded the bus and there were no seats in the front, the black riders were required to give up their seats for the white passenger. Also, after black passengers paid their fare at the front of the bus, many drivers made them get off the bus

*Scenes from the bus boycott: Parks being
fingerprinted in Montgomery (top); Parks in a
sheriff's department booking photo (center);
Parks being escorted up the courthouse
steps by E.D. Nixon (bottom).*

and board from the rear entrance. Some drivers would take off as the black passengers made their way around to the back entrance.

On that fateful day—Thursday, December 1, 1955—Rosa Parks took the bus home from work, as usual. Most days, she would check the driver before boarding. A Montgomery bus driver had evicted Parks from his bus 12 years earlier because, after paying her fare, she had walked through the bus instead of getting off the bus to board from the rear. Since then she tried to avoid his buses, but on that day in 1955 she boarded without noticing that it was the same driver. Parks took a seat in the first row of the black section. A white man boarded the bus, and because all of the seats in the white section were taken, the bus driver demanded that Parks and three other black passengers in her row move to the back. (At that time a black passenger couldn't even sit in the same row as a white, and the driver could change the boundaries of the white section to give seats to all the white passengers.) "Let me have those front seats," the driver said. "Y'all better make it light on yourselves and let me have those seats."

The other three black passengers moved, but Parks refused. She was tired of being humiliated, insulted, and treated as a second-class citizen. "People always say that I didn't give up my seat because I was tired, but that isn't true," she later declared. "I was not tired physically, or no more tired than I usually was at the end of a working day. I was not old, although some people have an image of me as being old then. I was 42. No, the only tired I was, was tired of giving in." As she said in her autobiography, "I had had enough. I wanted to be treated like a human being." When the bus driver threatened to have her arrested, she calmly told him, "You may do that." She was arrested, finger-printed, and put in jail.

"People always say that I didn't give up my seat because I was tired, but that isn't true. I was not tired physically, or no more tired than I usually was at the end of a working day. I was not old, although some people have an image of me as being old then. I was 42. No, the only tired I was, was tired of giving in."

Parks was not the first African American to be arrested for disobeying the bus segregation laws. In the previous year, several black women, including a 15-year-old girl, had been arrested for the same reason. The black community had talked in the past about staging a demonstration against the buses, but they were waiting for the right opportunity. When word got out that Rosa Parks had been arrested, they agreed this was the opportunity they had been waiting for. Parks was well respected in Montgomery, and black leaders felt that the community would rally around her case.

Several hours after her arrest, E.D. Nixon, president of the Alabama chapter of the NAACP, contacted the liberal white lawyer Clifford Durr for help. Those two, along with Durr's wife, Virginia, posted the $100 bond for Parks's release from jail. That night, they asked if she would be willing to challenge her arrest at her trial the following Monday. They would use her case to challenge the constitutionality of the bus segregation laws. It could be dangerous, but Parks agreed.

Over the weekend, leaders in the African-American community worked together to plan how to challenge the arrest. They decided to announce a bus boycott for Monday, December 5, the day of the trial. More than 35,000 flyers were distributed throughout Montgomery asking citizens to boycott the buses on the day of Parks's trial. The leaflet said, "Don't ride the buses to work, to town, to school, or anywhere on Monday." The boycott was publicized in a Montgomery newspaper and also in African-American churches that Sunday, as black preachers exhorted their congregants to stay off the buses on Monday.

_____ " _____

Martin Luther King Jr. gave a speech in front of thousands of African Americans who came to support the boycott: "There comes a time when people get tired of being trampled over by the iron feet of oppression.... We are here, we are here because we are tired now."

_____ " _____

THE MONTGOMERY BUS BOYCOTT

At her trial, Parks was found guilty of violating the state segregation laws. She was fined $10 plus the $4 court fees. But the bus boycott worked—it was so effective that 90 percent of blacks stayed off the buses that first day. And leaders of the boycott immediately began planning how to continue it.

That same night, a group of boycott supporters held a church rally and decided to continue the boycott. One of the preachers involved in the bus boycott was the young Reverend Martin Luther King Jr., who had only recently started preaching at the Dexter Avenue Baptist Church. He had been asked to lead the Montgomery Improvement Association, a group formed to direct the boycott. King gave a speech in front of thousands of African Americans who came to support the boycott. In his speech, King said, "There comes a time when people get tired of being trampled over by

Rev. Martin Luther King Jr. discusses strategies for the boycott with his advisors and organizers. Parks is seated in the front row, with fellow civil rights leader Rev. Ralph Abernathy to the left.

the iron feet of oppression. . . . We are here, we are here because we are tired now."

During the boycott, Parks herself spent time organizing carpools for those who chose to give up the buses. She also traveled around the country raising money to fund the boycott. It was a tremendous hardship for all involved. Some people managed to get rides to work, but many had to walk up to 20 miles each day. Boycott supporters were harassed, and both Rosa and Raymond Parks lost their jobs and were threatened.

For over a year, boycotters refused to ride the buses in Montgomery. This took a major financial toll on the bus companies, nearly bankrupting some. On February 1, 1956, the Montgomery Improvement Association, headed by Martin Luther King Jr., filed a lawsuit in the U.S. District Court stating that the Alabama segregation laws were unconstitutional. On June 2, the lower court agreed, declaring segregated seating on buses unconstitutional. The U.S. Supreme Court upheld the lower court order that Montgomery buses be integrated. Finally, on December 20, 1956, Montgomery officials were given a court order to end bus segregation. The boycott ended the next day, after 381 days. The success of the Montgomery bus boycott spurred blacks in other cities around the country to follow suit.

Some 30 years after the incident, Parks said, "At the time I was arrested, I had no idea it would turn into this. It was just a day like any other day. The only thing that made it significant was that the masses of the people joined in."

LIFE AFTER THE BOYCOTT

Life for Rosa did not get any easier during or after the boycott. She and Raymond were both fired from their jobs, and they were constantly threatened by white supremacists. Because of all the violence directed at them and other blacks in the community, Raymond suffered a nervous breakdown. In 1957, Rosa, Raymond, and Rosa's mother moved to Detroit, Michigan, where Rosa's brother lived. Rosa worked as a seamstress for several years. Then in 1965, Representative John Conyers, a member of the U.S. Congress, hired her to work in his office. Parks worked for Rep. Conyers until she retired in 1988.

In Detroit, Parks remained active in civil rights activities. She joined the NAACP and participated in peaceful demonstrations, including the 1963 March on Washington. She made public appearances with Dr. King. She was also involved in the Southern Christian Leadership Conference and served as a deaconess at the St. Matthew African Methodist Episcopal Church. She also spent much of her time working with youth groups and working to house the homeless in Michigan.

Raymond Parks died of cancer in 1977, but Rosa continued her work for equal rights. In 1987, she founded the Rosa and Raymond Parks Institute for Self-Development. This organization took children of different races around the country, traveling by bus, to learn about the civil rights movement.

In August 1994, a young unemployed black man broke into Parks's home and beat and robbed her. He knew who she was, but he was high on drugs and alcohol. Rather than condemn the man, Parks sympathized with him. She said, "I pray for this young man and the condition of our country that has made him this way."

For years after her refusal to give up her seat on the bus, Parks was recognized for her bravery. She received numerous awards over the years, including the Spingarn Medal, awarded in 1979 by the NAACP; the Medal of Freedom, awarded in 1996 by President Bill Clinton; the first International Freedom Conductor Award, awarded in 1998 by the National Underground Railroad Freedom Center; and the Gold Medal of Honor, awarded in 1999 by President Clinton and the United States Congress. This is the highest governmental award possible for an American civilian. For her contribution

Parks receiving the Medal of Freedom from President Bill Clinton
in the Oval Office of the White House, 1996.

to American ethnic diversity, Parks was one of 80 people to receive a medal of honor at the Statue of Liberty's 100th birthday celebration. Across the country, schools, streets, and libraries have been named after her. She is discussed in virtually all U.S. history books, and children around the country learn about her courageous act.

Toward the end of the 1990s, Parks made fewer and fewer public appearances. Her health was worsening, and she began to develop dementia. In April 1999, her attorneys filed a lawsuit against the rap group OutKast for using her name without consent in their 1998 song "Rosa Parks." Some of her legal representatives felt that the song exploited her, but the members of OutKast explained that they meant to honor her and thank for her civil rights work. (For more information on OutKast, see *Biography Today*, Sep. 2004.) The case was finally settled in April 2005. As part of the settlement, the group and the record label agreed to help produce a tribute album about Parks.

In December 2000, the Rosa Parks Library and Museum was opened in Montgomery, Alabama, in the exact spot where she sat on the bus. The library and museum cover 50,000 square feet and include a life-sized bronze sculpture of Parks.

On December 1, 2005, President George W. Bush signed bill HR 4145, giving Congress approval to place a statue of Rosa Parks in Statuary Hall,

Mourners stood in line for hours to file past the casket of Rosa Parks as it rested in honor in the Rotunda of the U.S. Capitol Building in Washington, DC, October 31, 2005.

which is next to the Capitol Rotunda in Washington, DC. This made her the first African-American woman to be honored with a statue in the Capitol. During the signing ceremony, Bush said, "It is fitting that this American hero will now be honored with a monument inside the most visible symbol of American democracy. We hope that generations of Americans will remember what this brave woman did and be inspired to add their own contributions to the unfolding story of American freedom for all."

SAYING GOOD BYE TO ROSA PARKS

Rosa Parks died peacefully in her home in Detroit, Michigan, on October 24, 2005. Her longtime assistant, Elaine Steele, said that, "She was peaceful. She passed away in her sleep." News of Parks's death brought together many people from all over the country. Because she was such an influential figure in American history, three separate funerals were held in her honor.

On October 29, 2005, Rosa Parks's body was brought to Montgomery, Alabama. Southwest Airlines donated a commercial flight to transport her casket from Detroit to Montgomery. Lou Freeman, the first black chief pilot to fly for a major airline, donated his time, as did his crew, to bring her to Alabama. The funeral was held at the St. Paul African American Episcopal Church, where thousands of mourners, young and old alike, lined up to say good-bye. Many drove from miles away and stood in line for hours to catch a glimpse of the legendary Rosa Parks. During the service, Bobby Bright, mayor of Montgomery, told the crowd that there had been talk of giving an official pardon to Parks for her act of defiance 50 years earlier. He said that instead, he would like to "ask that Mrs. Rosa Parks pardon us. Pardon us for the way we treated her." Secretary of State Condoleezza Rice said, "I think I can quite honestly say that if it were not for Rosa Parks, I would not be standing here today. It is really the actions and courage of individuals that matter, and this woman mattered." Other speakers included Oprah Winfrey, Dorothy I. Height, president emerita of the National Council of Negro Women, and Melvin Watt , Chair of the Congressional Black Caucus. Over 20,000 people came to pay respects at her viewing.

On October 30, 2005, Rosa Parks's body was brought to Washington, DC. Not only did she make history when she was alive, but she also made history after her death. She became the first woman to lie in honor in the Rotunda of the U.S. Capitol Building in Washington, DC. She was also the second African American and the 30th American in the nation's history to have this honor.

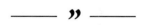

"If it were not for Rosa Parks, I would not be standing here today," said Secretary of State Condoleezza Rice. "It is really the actions and courage of individuals that matter, and this woman mattered."

People from across the country came to say good-bye to this prominent civil rights activist. The line of mourners waiting to walk past the casket took several hours just to reach the Rotunda. As they walked by her casket, many people thanked Parks for what she did in 1955. Early the next morning, the wait was still estimated to be five hours long. Officials said that they would keep the Capitol open as long as it took.

Many dignitaries attended the memorial service at the Capitol building. Approximately 500 people crowded inside the Rotunda for the memorial service. President George W. Bush and First Lady Laura Bush presented the presidential wreath for the center of the casket.

Parks's body was then brought to Detroit, Michigan, her final resting place. Her body lay in state at the Charles H. Wright Museum of African American History. Approximately 8,000 people stood in the rain to wait for her arrival. More than 75,000 people visited Parks at the museum.

On the day of her funeral, the first row in hundreds of Detroit buses was left empty to honor Rosa Parks's memory. Many VIPs attended the service at the Greater Grace Temple, including former President Bill Clinton, Rev. Jesse Jackson, Rev. Al Sharpton, and Louis Farrakhan. President Clinton was the first to speak. He said that Rosa Parks was worthy of honor and praise because "her single simple act of dignity and courage struck a lethal blow to the foundations of legal bigotry. . . . Let us not forget [Rosa's] simple act. In a lifetime of grace and dignity, she made us see and agree that everyone should be free." Detroit Mayor Kwame Kilpatrick said that because of Rosa Parks, "a little chubby kid on the west side of Detroit grew to believe he could be anything he wanted to be." He continued, "Thank you for sacrificing for us. Thank you for praying when we were too cool and too cute to pray for ourselves. . . . Thank you for allowing us to step on your mighty shoulders." Other speakers at the service included Senator Hillary Clinton; Bruce Gordon, head of the NAACP; Marc H. Morial, president of the National Urban League; Jennifer Granholm, Governor of Michigan; Senator John Kerry; and many more. The service was scheduled to last three hours, but it lasted more than seven hours.

——— " ———

"Rosa Parks has shown the awesome power of right over might in history's long journey for peace and freedom," said Rev. Jesse Jackson. "She sat down in order that we might stand up. Paradoxically, her imprisonment opened the doors for our long journey to freedom."

——— " ———

After the funeral, Parks's casket was transported to Detroit's Woodlawn Cemetery. Before her body was brought into the cemetery's mausoleum, 152 doves were released, a U.S. Marine played the bagpipes, and there was a 21-gun salute.

THE LEGACY OF ROSA PARKS

Although few people knew her personally at the time of her death, Rosa Parks touched the lives of many Americans. In honoring and remembering her, public figures around the United States praised her for her role in changing the country.

Coretta Scott King, widow of Martin Luther King Jr., said that "by sheer force of her will, she set in motion a revolution that continues to reverberate in nation after nation and remains an inspiration to liberation movements everywhere." Their daughter, Reverend Bernice King, said that Rosa Parks "was the catalyst of one of the most important freedom movements, not only in American history, but in the world history. . . . Indeed she became the symbol and personification of our nonviolent struggle for liberation and human dignity."

The District of Columbia Honor Guard showing respect for the memory of Rosa Parks.

Senator Barack Obama from Illinois called Parks a national hero. "Through her courage and by her example, she helped lay the foundation for a country that could begin to live up to its creed," Obama said. "Just as important, she reminded each and every one of us of our personal responsibilities to stand up for what is right and the central truth of the American experience that our greatness as a nation derives from seemingly ordinary people doing extraordinary things." He also said that Parks was a woman who "held no public office, she wasn't a wealthy woman, didn't appear in the society pages. And yet when the history of this country is written, it is this small, quiet woman whose name will be remembered long after the names of senators and presidents have been forgotten."

Poet Rita Dove, former U.S. Poet Laureate and winner of the 1987 Pulitzer Prize for Poetry, maintained that Parks was an example for all people. "It is the modesty of Rosa Parks's example that sustains us," Dove affirmed. "It is no less than the belief in the power of the individual, that cornerstone of the American dream, that she inspires, along with the hope that all of us—even the least of us—could be that brave, that serenely human, when crunch time comes."

Perhaps Rev. Jesse Jackson best summed up the legacy of Rosa Parks. "With quiet courage and nonnegotiable dignity, Rosa Parks was an activist and a freedom fighter who transformed a nation and confirmed a notion that ordinary people can have an extraordinary effect on the world," said Jackson.

"Rosa Parks has shown the awesome power of right over might in history's long journey for peace and freedom. She sat down in order that we might stand up. Paradoxically, her imprisonment opened the doors for our long journey to freedom."

HONORS AND AWARDS

Spingarn Medal (NAACP): 1979
Martin Luther King Jr. Award: 1980
Martin Luther King Jr Nonviolent Peace Prize: 1980
Eleanor Roosevelt Women of Courage Award (Wonder Woman
    Foundation): 1984
Martin Luther King Jr. Leadership Award: 1987
Medal of Freedom: 1996
International Freedom Conductor Award (National Underground
    Railroad Freedom Center): 1998
Congressional Gold Medal of Honor: 1999

WRITINGS

The Autobiography of Rosa Parks, 1990, reprinted as *Rosa Parks:
    My Story*, 1992 (with Jim Haskins)
*Quiet Strength: The Faith, the Hope, and the Heart of a Woman Who
    Changed a Nation*, 1994 (with Gregory J. Reed)
Dear Mrs. Parks: A Dialogue with Today's Youth, 1996
    (with Gregory J. Reed)
I Am Rosa Parks, 1997 (with Gregory J. Reed)

FURTHER READING

Books

Biography Today, 1992; 1994 (Update)
Contemporary Authors, Vol. 150, 1996
Contemporary Authors, New Revision Series, Vol. 102, 2002
Contemporary Black Biography, Vol. 35, 2002
Encyclopedia of World Biography, 1998
Hull, Mary. *Rosa Parks*, 1994 (juvenile)
Notable Black American Women, Vol. 1, 1992
Parks, Rosa, with Jim Haskins. *Rosa Parks: My Story*, 1992
Who's Who among African Americans, 2005
Who's Who in America, 2006

Periodicals

Chicago Tribune, Oct. 25, 2005, p.1
Current Biography Yearbook, 1989

Ebony, Jan. 2006, p.126
Economist, Oct. 29, 2005, Obituary
Jet, Nov. 21, 2005, p.6
New York Times, Nov. 3, 2005, p.A16
Time, June 14, 1999
Washington Post, Oct. 31, 2005, p.A1

Online Articles

http://www.cnn.com/2005/US/10/24/parks.obit
 (CNN, "Civil Rights Icon Rosa Parks Dies at 92," Oct. 25, 2005)
http://www.npr.org/templates/story/story.php?storyId=4973548&
 sourceCode=gaw
 (NPR, "Civil Rights Icon Rosa Parks Dies," Oct. 25, 2005)
http://www.time.com/time/time100/heroes/profile/parks01.html
 (*Time,* Heroes and Icons, "Rosa Parks: Her Simple Act of Protest
 Galvanized America's Civil Rights Revolution," June 14, 1999)
http://www.washingtonpost.com/wp-dyn/content/article/2005/10/24/
 AR2005102402053_pf.html
 (*Washington Post,* "Bus Ride Shook a Nation's Conscience,"
 Oct. 25, 2005)

Online Databases

Biography Resource Center Online, 2006, articles from *Contemporary
 Authors Online,* 2005; *Contemporary Black Biography,* 2002;
 Encyclopedia of World Biography, 1998; and *Who's Who among
 African Americans,* 2005

WORLD WIDE WEB SITES

http://www.rosaparks.org
http://teacher.scholastic.com/rosa

Danica Patrick 1982-

American Race Car Driver
2005 Bombardier Rookie of the Year in the
Indy Racing League
First Female Driver to Lead the Indy 500

BIRTH

Danica Sue Patrick was born on March 25, 1982, in Beloit, Wisconsin. She has one younger sister, Brooke. Patrick's parents, T. J. and Bev, met at a snowmobile race where T. J. was a competitor and Bev was a mechanic. Danica and her sister grew up in Roscoe, Illinois, a suburb of the city of Rockford. Her parents owned a glass installation business and a coffee shop.

YOUTH

Patrick and her family agree that when she was a youngster, she had little interest in cars or driving. "She was a girlie girl," recalled her mother. "She didn't want to get grease under her fingernails." Instead, she liked to play and dream of a career as a veterinarian, a singer, or a secretary. All of that changed at age 10, though, when Patrick went with Brooke to a go-kart race. "I didn't want to get left out, so I went ahead and tried it, too," Patrick recalled.

Go-karts are popular vehicles that children and adults can drive at many theme parks or courses especially made for the pastime. The karts are usually confined to small tracks surrounded by walls of rubber tires. But go-karting is also a popular amateur sport, with local and national circuits for people who want to compete in races.

Patrick's debut as a racer was hardly promising. Her brakes failed, which led to a bruising crash. Even worse, she got "lapped" (passed) twice within the first six laps of the race. Nevertheless, the sport took hold of her imagination. Her younger sister decided not to pursue racing, but Patrick was so captivated that she entered a local junior racing league. With the support, coaching, and encouragement of her father, she improved quickly and finished second in

—— " ——

"You have to find your passion in life," Patrick said. "I grew up in a family where I was never told I can't do anything."

—— " ——

points at the end of the 22-race season. "I loved the way you could see yourself get better in racing," she told *Sports Illustrated*. "I might finish a second and a half ahead of everyone, but it was never good enough. I could always be better."

With each passing month, Patrick learned more from her father about the mechanics of go-karts and the strategies for developing physical and mental toughness. The family also invested money and time getting her to both local and national go-kart competitions. Patrick later credited this support as a major factor in her racing success. "You have to find your passion in life," she explained. "I grew up in a family where I was never told I can't do anything." Outside observers noticed her family's support as well. "All the funding that could have gone to a nice home and vacations for the family went into Danica's racing," former race car driver Lyn St. James said. "Her younger sister was there to polish the car. So not only did you have talent, drive, and determination, you had everything you need to have [to succeed]."

Two years after her first race, the 12-year-old Patrick won her first national points championship from the World Karting Association (WKA), Yamaha

Patrick standing by her car before qualifying for a June 2003 race in Monterey, California.

Sportsman class. Meanwhile, she won both the Yamaha Sportsman and the US820 Sportsman championships while competing in a local circuit called the Great Lakes Sprint Series. In 1996, at age 14, Patrick won 39 of the 49 feature races she entered, earning WKA national points titles in both Junior and Restricted Junior classes. One year later, in her final full season of go-karting, she captured the WKA Grand National Championship, HPV class.

By this time, Patrick was routinely beating older male drivers. One key to her success was that she refused to let them intimidate her, despite her small stature and youth. During one indoor go-kart practice run in Florida, for example, a 30-year-old male driver twice rammed into her tires after she had lapped him three times in a matter of minutes. Patrick retaliated by stepping on the gas and slamming the driver into the wall. "After the race, he came up and punched her in the helmet," recalled a witness. "So she punched him right back, as if to say, 'No one messes with me.' I don't think the guy realized she was a girl because her helmet was on. I think when he saw all that brown hair fall out of it, he just about died.'"

EDUCATION

Patrick faced some tough decisions as her racing career expanded. During her years at Hononegah Community High School, for example, she tried to participate in normal activities such as volleyball, choir, and cheerleading while simultaneously competing in go-kart races around the country. As time passed, however, she decided that she could not stay in school and still pursue the racing career she wanted. She dropped out during her junior year of high school, although she later earned a GED (general equivalency diploma).

Patrick's decision to leave school early was due in part to the encouragement she received from her mentor Lyn St. James, a former Indy driver and one of only four women to compete in the Indianapolis 500. St. James saw budding talent in Patrick, who trained for about two years in her driving school. "Out of the 200 that have gone through my program, no more than 10 set themselves apart that I've gone out of my way to help behind the scenes," St. James said. "They have to be exceptional. It's not good enough to just be good. The reality is you have to be extraordinary. I saw Danica as extraordinary."

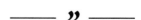

"Out of the 200 that have gone through my program, no more than 10 set themselves apart that I've gone out of my way to help behind the scenes," said Lyn St. James, a former Indy driver who now runs a driving school where Patrick trained. "They have to be exceptional. It's not good enough to just be good. The reality is you have to be extraordinary. I saw Danica as extraordinary."

CAREER HIGHLIGHTS

In 1998 the 16-year-old Patrick made the dramatic decision to try her racing luck in England, which boasted competitive racing leagues that attracted promising young drivers from around the world, "If you want to be the best lawyer, you go to Harvard," her mother later explained. "If you want to be the best driver, you go to England."

Leaving her family behind, Patrick relocated to Milton Keyes, England, and joined the extremely competitive Formula Vauxhall Series, sponsored by the United Kingdom's Vauxhall Motor Company. Most of the Vauxhall races are on demanding open roads or courses with irregular curves. In 1999—her first full season with Formula Vauxhall—Patrick finished ninth in the Formula Vauxhall Championship. The next year she earned a spot with England's Zetek Formula Ford series, considered one of the toughest proving grounds for young drivers. Patrick excelled on the circuit, and her second-place finish at the prestigious Formula Ford Festival in 2000 was the best-ever showing by an American *or* a female driver in the history of the event.

Patrick later recalled that the years she spent racing in England—first in Formula Vauxhall, later in Formula Ford—were the most difficult of her life. "I know that England changed me a bit," she admitted. "I know I became a little bit colder, a little different. . . . What doesn't kill you makes you stronger. It was tough, but it's made me what I am today. I hope people like it. If they don't, this is me. I'm very true to myself and true to my personality."

Patrick's performance in England gained her the respect and attention of racing giants like Bobby Rahal, a former Indianapolis 500 winner and the co-owner (with talk show host David Letterman) of the Rahal-Letterman racing team, one of the top teams in the Indy Racing League (IRL). "When you race in England as a young person, there's no quarter given there," Rahal later said. "It's a hostile environment, and it's even more hostile for a woman, or a young girl. If you're a guy, you can go out with the guys and drink beer. What's a girl supposed to do? That spoke volumes in my mind about what she was all about."

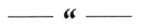

"I know that England changed me a bit," Patrick said. "I know I became a little bit colder, a little different.... What doesn't kill you makes you stronger. It was tough, but it's made me what I am today."

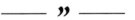

Signing with Team Rahal-Letterman

In 2001 Patrick won the Gorsline Scholarship Award for top upcoming road race driver. This accomplishment further intrigued Rahal. He recognized that she was competing on open road courses rather than banked oval tracks such as those found in the IRL, but he liked her determination and her mental toughness. In 2002 he signed her to a multi-year contract with Team Rahal-Letterman, confident that she could prepare herself to compete on the Indy Racing League (IRL) circuit.

Even with all her years of European experience, Patrick had to learn more before she entered the big leagues. She began 2002 with the Barber Dodge Pro Series, running a limited schedule of five races. Patrick immediately showed that she belonged. In her debut in Toronto, Ontario, she qualified 11th but finished seventh in the race. Her best showing with Barber Dodge came on July 28, 2002, when she finished fourth in a race in Vancouver, British Columbia. Pleased with her accomplishments, Rahal announced that he would promote her to the Toyota Atlantic Series for her first full season in American racing.

As the 2003 racing season progressed, Patrick proved that Rahal's confidence in her was justified. She posted top-five finishes in five races and earned two podium (top three) finishes: one in Monterrey, Mexico, and one in the season finale in Miami, Florida. These finishes marked the first two times in the 30-year history of the Atlantic Series that a female driver had earned a spot on the podium.

Patrick returned to the Toyota Atlantic Series in 2004. She was the only driver that season to compete in every lap of every race. Not surprisingly, she posted another strong year. She made history as the first woman driver to win a pole position (the lead position at the beginning of a race) for a Toyota Atlantic event, and by season's end she had earned three podium visits. Overall, she compiled an impressive 10 top-five finishes in 12 races. Her third-place finish at the Toyota Atlantic Championship was the best ever for a female in the series. For a time she led the series in points, also a first for a female driver.

Joining the IndyCar Series

Despite her success, though, Patrick was shocked when Rahal announced on December 8, 2004, that she would become the third teammate on the Rahal-Letterman IRL IndyCar Series. She had made it to the top level of Indy racing. Only three other women had advanced to the famous series before Patrick: Janet Guthrie (1977), Lyn St. James (1992), and Sarah Fisher (2000). None of those three had the top-flight equipment and support at Patrick's command, however. This support, combined with her self-confidence and her attractive physical appearance, led many observers to wonder if a new star had arrived on the IRL circuit.

"When you race in England as a young person, there's no quarter given there," said Bobby Rahal, a former Indy 500 winner. "It's a hostile environment, and it's even more hostile for a woman, or a young girl. If you're a guy, you can go out with the guys and drink beer. What's a girl supposed to do? That spoke volumes in my mind about what she was all about."

Team Rahal-Letterman provided Patrick with a first-class car for her rookie campaign: a pioneer No. 16 Panoz/Honda/Firestone (Panoz is the chassis, or body of the car; Honda made the engine; and the car was outfitted with Firestone tires). Patrick used the first four races of the 2005 season to become accustomed to her new ride, then found herself staring in the face of her first Indianapolis 500—only her fifth race with the IRL, and her first at the distance of 500 miles.

Oval-track races consist of two events. First the drivers must qualify. That means they must drive alone around the track at the highest speed they

*Patrick during the 2005 Indy 500, where she became
the first woman to lead at Indy.*

can achieve. The fastest driver gets the pole position. When all the qualifying drivers are ranked, their starting positions in the race have been determined. Only a limited number of spots are open, though, so some drivers miss the cut entirely and are relegated to the sidelines for the race.

Incredibly, Patrick claimed the fourth spot in the entire field during qualifying by posting an average speed of 227.004 miles per hour—a spectacular showing for a rookie driver. This performance increased the attention swirling around her from sports broadcasters and journalists. Although she admitted to having "3,000 knots" in her stomach, Patrick faced the media with grace and promised she would live up to her hype when the race began.

Making an Impact at Indy

On Sunday, May 29, 2005, the 89th running of the Indianapolis 500 began when an announcer said, "Lady and gentlemen, start your engines." A few moments later, the green starting flag was waved and Patrick and her fellow drivers roared forward before a crowd of more than 300,000 and a national television audience.

Patrick drove steadily during the early part of the race. She kept her fourth-place spot until she entered the pits on the 78th lap. In what she later described as a "rookie mistake," she stalled while trying to re-enter the race.

The blunder dropped her to 16th place. Then, at lap 155, she spun on a turn and hit another racer. The accident damaged the front of her Panoz/Honda, forcing her to make another trip to the pit for a new nose cone. The pit crew repaired the damage in one minute, and she returned to the race.

Just four laps later, Patrick entered the pits again, to fill her tank with fuel and get new tires. She had 41 laps left to drive in the race, and Rahal decided to "roll the dice" and have her try to stay on the track and conserve fuel. He knew that the drivers ahead of Patrick in the race at that point would all need to pit for fuel at least one more time. If Patrick conserved her gas and drove smoothly, she had a shot at winning the race and making Indy 500 history.

The gamble appeared to pay off, as one by one the drivers ahead of her pulled in to pit row for fuel. Patrick kept roaring around the track at an average speed of 225 miles per hour, and at Lap 172 she claimed first place in the 200-lap race.

"[Danica Patrick] single-handedly injected the 89th running of the Indianapolis 500 with the sort of voltage it knew back in the day," declared sportswriter E. M. Swift.

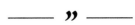

One big question loomed: Would Patrick have enough fuel in her car to finish the race? She had to slow her speed to conserve the remaining gas. She knew that caution flags—which require drivers to slow down so that track officials can clear accidents from the track—would help her cause, but the caution flag only came out once during the final laps of the race. In the end the racers were running full throttle, and Patrick was passed on the 194th lap by veteran British driver Dan Wheldon, who eventually won the race. Two other drivers passed Patrick as well, pushing her to a fourth-place finish.

Patrick was a little disappointed that she had been unable to pull off a storybook victory in her first Indianapolis 500. But her performance had changed the history of Indy racing forever. She became the first woman ever to run in the lead in the Indianapolis 500, the first woman to finish in the top five, and the first to be considered a serious contender for victory. "[Danica Patrick] single-handedly injected the 89th running of the Indianapolis 500 with the sort of voltage it knew back in the day," declared sportswriter E. M. Swift.

The New Face of Indy Racing?

In the days following the 2005 Indy 500, it was clear that Patrick had captured the imagination of the national media. Patrick appeared on the cover of

Patrick, shown here signing autographs for racing fans, became one of the most popular drivers in the Indy Racing League (IRL) during her rookie campaign.

Sports Illustrated—the first Indy car driver to be so honored since 1981. She did a full round of television appearances and was featured in *People, Us Weekly,* and *TV Guide* magazines. In addition, several companies approached her with commercial endorsement proposals. Before long, Patrick had agreed to promote a variety of products in TV commercials and print advertising in exchange for millions of dollars in fees.

Corporate America's interest in Patrick stemmed from its recognition that she was, in the words of E. M. Swift, a "5'1", 100-pound package of marketing gold." Not only was she a talented, aggressive driver, she was also beautiful, poised, and willing to sell her sport. For more than a decade, the IRL has lost fans to the more popular NASCAR series, a racing league that uses regular automobile chassis rather than the sleek, open-wheeled Indy cars. Since her 2005 debut with the IRL, however, Patrick has generated significantly higher TV ratings for Indy events.

Patrick's presence has also been cited as an important factor in attracting new fans to IRL races. "Danica" merchandise sells briskly at events and in stores, and reporters have coined the term "Danicamania" to describe the media frenzy that surrounds her at races. "Like a Tiger Woods, Patrick not only gets props for her talent but attracts the eyes of those who care little about sports," wrote Michelle Hiskey. "She's got a fresh face, guts, and a good Midwestern story of gumption. If anyone can reverse the dipping popularity of open-wheel racing, it's she."

Racing in a Man's World

Patrick appreciates her expanding fan base and her rising popularity. But the recognition she treasures most, though, concerns her on-track performance. Patrick finished her rookie season ranked 12th in points out of a field of 36 drivers, an impressive showing for a first-year participant. At the end of the 2005 IRL season, Patrick was named IRL Indy Car Rookie of the Year.

Are the male racers in the Indy series jealous of Patrick's share of the limelight? Most of them are very grateful that she has entered the league. Her popularity has helped spark renewed interest in open-wheeled racing and has attracted new fans, especially women. "She's going to bring everybody around," said fellow racer Helio Castroneves. "Everybody is going to benefit from [her popularity]. Hopefully, she will take advantage of it. Hopefully, we will take advantage of it. It's just great. I'm a big fan of hers."

"I absolutely want the success more than anything," Patrick said. "My goal is not to be the first female to do things, and it's not to be a poster child or a calendar girl. It's just to win."

A few fellow drivers have complained that Patrick's weight—a mere 100 pounds—gives her an unfair advantage behind the wheel. They suggest that the lighter a car is, the faster it can run. Patrick counters that the 2004 Indianapolis 500 was won by the heaviest car on the track, and that her weight has nothing to do with how her vehicles perform.

Patrick has many advantages as she looks into her future. She is young and still learning the finer points of race management. She has the best equipment to use, a winning veteran driver, Bobby Rahal, as a coach, and the respect of the men she races against. "I absolutely want the success more than anything," she clarified. "My goal is not to be the first female to do things, and it's not to be a poster child or a calendar girl. It's just to win."

MARRIAGE AND FAMILY

On November 19, 2005, Patrick married Paul Hospenthal in a quiet ceremony in Scottsdale, Arizona. She met Hospenthal, a physical therapist, when he began treating her for a hip ailment. The couple has no plans to start a family at this time, since that would interfere with Patrick's career. When not racing, she lives in Arizona.

HOBBIES AND OTHER INTERESTS

Patrick is a serious athlete who is very careful about what she eats and how she exercises. "They've done tests on drivers, and their heart rate can stay at 180 beats per minute for like two hours, which is incredibly demanding," she explained. "Every time you turn the wheel side to side, you can feel everything from your neck and shoulders down to your lower back working." Patrick exercises every day to keep in shape for driving. She lifts weights several times a week, and practices yoga for balance and flexibility.

HONORS AND AWARDS

Grand National Champion, Yamaha Class (World Karting Association): 1994
Manufacturers' Cup, Yamaha Sportsman Class (World Karting Association): 1994
National Points Title, Yamaha Junior and Restricted Junior Classes (World Karting Association): 1996
Grand National Champion, Yamaha Lite and HPV Classes (World Karting Association): 1997
Gorsline Scholarship Award: 2001
IRL Rookie of the Year (Indy Racing League): 2005

FURTHER READING

Books

Ingram, Jonathan. *Danica Patrick: America's Hottest Racer,* 2005
Who's Who in America, 2006

Periodicals

Auto Week, Jan. 28, 2002, p.38
Chicago Sun-Times, May 29, 2005, p.122
Chicago Tribune, Mar. 10, 2005, p.2; July 20, 2005, p.C1
Current Biography Yearbook, 2005
Muscle and Fitness, Nov. 2003, p.31
New York Daily News, Sep. 22, 2005
New York Times, May 30, 2005, p.A3; May 31, 2005, p.D1; June 3, 2005, p.D1; June 12, 2005, p.8
People, June 6, 2005, p.126
Sports Illustrated, Sep. 2, 2002, p.14; June 6, 2005, p.54; June 20, 2005, p.87; Dec.12, 2005, p.96

Sports Illustrated for Kids, Aug. 2005, p.13
Time, June 13, 2005, p.6

Online Databases

Biography Resource Center Online, 2006

ADDRESS

Danica Patrick
Rahal Letterman Racing
4601 Lyman Drive
Columbus, OH 43026

WORLD WIDE WEB SITES

http://www.danicaracing.com
http://www.indyracingleague.com
http://www.rahal.com/drivers/patrick/index.jsp

Jorge Ramos 1958-
Mexican Journalist
Anchorman for Univision's Spanish-Language
News Broadcasts

BIRTH

Jorge Ramos was born on March 16, 1958, in a lower middle-class neighborhood of Mexico City, Mexico. His father, also named Jorge, was an architect, and his mother, Lourdes, looked after the family. The eldest in a family of five children, Ramos has three brothers, Alejandro, Eduardo, and Gerardo. He also has one sister, Lourdes, who works as a television journalist in Mexico.

YOUTH

Ramos was raised in a tight-knit family. "My mother was the one who lent emotional support and my father the one who imposed discipline, though those who really got to know him knew that deep down my father was a softie," recalled Ramos. Although his father was an architect, he struggled to find work during long stretches because the nation's building construction industry was so weak. As a result, the family had to be very careful about spending money. In his autobiographical memoir *No Borders: A Journalist's Search for Home*, Ramos recalled that his parents could only afford to take the family out to a nice restaurant once or twice a year. "We lived right on the border of the middle class," was how he described their situation.

Despite his descriptions of tight economic times, Ramos also has many fond childhood memories. He and his siblings were surrounded by a large and supportive family, and he came to know both sets of grandparents. He also liked to roam the neighborhood, looking for swimming invitations from neighbors who owned swimming pools. When his neighbors went swimming, he recalled in *No Borders*, "my brothers and I would climb up on the wall surrounding their property so they would see us, hoping they would feel some pity and thereby extend an invitation to go swimming. It was healthy envy."

"My mother was the one who lent emotional support and my father the one who imposed discipline, though those who really got to know him knew that deep down my father was a softie," recalled Ramos.

Like many other Mexican boys, Ramos also loved soccer. In fact, he became so skilled at the sport that his neighborhood friends nicknamed him "Borjita Ramos," after a famous player on the Mexican national team. According to Ramos, soccer was "what divided the world; on the one hand were those who knew how to play, and on the other . . . everyone else."

Ramos's dexterity abandoned him when it came time to learn practical skills, though. "Hammering nails or fixing a simple problem with an electric appliance was a virtually impossible task for me to do," he recalled. "I am the exact opposite of a handyman." When it became clear that he would not grow up to be an engineer, as his father had initially hoped, Ramos made a special effort to develop other skills. He decided, for example, that writing and debating skills "would allow me to compensate for my lack of understanding of the machines that surround me." He also became a talented classical guitar player. He trained for eight years, and at the age of 12 he appeared on television in a guitar competition.

EDUCATION

From kindergarten through high school, Ramos was sent away from home to attend Catholic schools run by Benedictine priests. His first school was the Colegio Tepeyac (later renamed the Centro Escolar del Lago) on the outskirts of Mexico City. "I never had any academic problems," he recalled. "I didn't need to study much to get good grades." He also became such a poised public speaker from an early age that he bragged that he could talk his way through any class presentation.

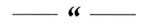

> "That night, at home in the kitchen, I told my mother [about my spinal condition], and I began to cry like never before," Ramos recalled. "So many years, so much hard work and so many plans, all in vain."

Not surprisingly, Ramos's favorite part of school was recess, when he could play soccer and basketball with his friends. But he deeply disliked the Benedictine priests who ran the school. "[They] used their position of authority and their supposed heavenly contacts to try and fill our heads, using blood, shouts, punishment, and fear, with their reactionary ideas," he charged. He later claimed that the priests instilled an unhealthy fear of hell and the devil in him and some of his other classmates. Ramos also came to feel that the priests favored unnecessarily cruel punishments against students who broke their rules.

As he matured and grew more confident, Ramos rejected the organized religion of the priests, declaring that he "wanted nothing to do with the god that they represented." In its place, he developed his own personal form of spirituality and strived to live an honest and decent life. As Ramos explained in *No Borders*, his experience in Catholic school turned him into "an agnostic who wanted to be a believer."

Attending an Olympic Training School

When he was 14, Ramos entered a very different kind of school, the Centro Deportivo Olimpico Mexicano. This school works to prepare student athletes who have the potential to make the Mexican Olympic team. Ramos had always dreamed of representing his country in the Olympics as a runner or a high jumper. Though he did not demonstrate exceptional talent in either event as a teen, he wrote such a convincing letter to a member of the Olympic Committee that he was given a place at the school.

Once enrolled, Ramos began training for the high jump, but a seemingly minor back injury forced him to switch to running the hurdles. Strong showings in several national competitions gave him hope that he might qualify for the Olympic team in 1976 or 1980. But the back injury kept getting worse, and medical tests revealed that one of the vertebrae in his spinal column had not completely formed. When the doctors told him that the condition would prevent him from ever fulfilling his Olympic dream, Ramos was crushed. "That night, at home in the kitchen, I told my mother, and I began to cry like never before," he recalled in his memoir. "So many years, so much hard work, and so many plans, all in vain." He reluctantly obeyed the doctors and stopped training for the Olympics. Ever since then, though, he has remained a dedicated runner and recreational soccer player, and fortunately his spinal condition improved over time.

Deterred from his dreams of a career as an athlete, Ramos entered Universidad Iberoamericano (Latin American University) in Mexico City in 1977. It was the first school he attended for which he did not have a scholarship to pay his way, so he juggled his classroom responsibilities with a part-time job at a travel agency. He also decided to pursue studies in communication and psychology. He did not know quite what he would do following such studies, but he knew that he loved to study ideas and philosophy and to discuss such issues with his growing circle of

—— **"** ——

"Journalism did not interest me then," Ramos said about his early years in college. "'I don't like to chase after people,' I told my friends who had already started to fall under the journalistic spell. 'I prefer to make news, not cover it.' It wouldn't be long before I would have to eat my words."

—— **"** ——

friends. "Journalism did not interest me then," he admitted in *No Borders*. "'I don't like to chase after people,' I told my friends who had already started to fall under the journalistic spell. 'I prefer to make news, not cover it.' It wouldn't be long before I would have to eat my words." He graduated in 1981, earning a bachelor's degree with honors in communication.

Ramos later returned to school. He took journalism classes at the University of California at Los Angeles (UCLA) from 1983 to 1984, earning a professional designation in journalism. He also attended the University of Miami from 1993 to 1995, earning a master's degree in international studies.

FIRST JOBS

Ramos's first experiments with journalism stemmed from a basic need for money for tuition and living expenses. When he took a part-time job

Ramos during an interview with Cuban leader Fidel Castro in 1991 in Guadalajara, Mexico. According to Ramos, "When I asked him about the lack of democracy in Cuba, his bodyguards took me aside and pushed me away."

in the newsroom of a local radio station so that he could afford groceries, he was surprised to find that the work actually appealed to him. As he gained more experience, he gradually became convinced that he wanted to explore a career in television journalism. His big break came on March 30, 1981, when an assassination attempt was made on U.S. President Ronald Reagan. The radio station wanted to send someone to Washington, DC, to cover the story, and Ramos was the only journalist in the office who had both a reasonable command of English and a passport and visa that allowed him to travel.

Partly on the strength of the experience he gained covering the Reagan shooting, Ramos was able to make the leap to television when he returned to Mexico City a few weeks later. He accepted a position as an investigative journalist for the Mexican television station Televisa later that year. He quickly became disillusioned with the job, however. Televisa and the Mexican government both heavily censored his reports on official corruption and abuses of power.

In Mexico, the Partido Revolucionario Institucional (PRI) exerted the kind of political control that is unknown in the United States. Candidates for local office were hand-picked by the party, and the party demanded loyalty and obedience from all media sources, including television. The directors of one Mexican news show named "60 Minutes"—not to be confused with the news show of the same name in the United States—instructed Ramos to delete elements of a story he had submitted that were critical of the PRI. When he made only minor changes, the directors of the show ordered someone else to re-write it and then pressured Ramos to present the censored story on the air.

The experience was too much for a young man who was becoming deeply committed to ideas of press freedom and independence. Ramos resigned his position, writing that "what was asked of me goes against my honesty, principles, and professionalism." He also declared that the directors' actions amounted to "an assault on the most simple and clear idea of what journalism is: a search for truth."

Ramos decided that he would have to relocate to the United States to pursue his dreams of independent journalism. "Mexico in the early 1980s was suffocating me," he later stated in his memoirs. "If I had remained in Mexico, I would probably have been a poor, censored, frustrated journalist, or maybe a psychologist or university professor speaking out eternally and pathetically against those who censored me."

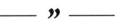

"Mexico in the early 1980s was suffocating me," Ramos wrote. *"If I had remained in Mexico, I would probably have been a poor, censored, frustrated journalist, or maybe a psychologist or university professor speaking out eternally and pathetically against those who censored me."*

In January 1983 Ramos left Mexico. He moved to California, where he took courses in television and journalism at the University of California-Los Angeles (UCLA). He rented a small room in a rambling house near the UCLA campus and bought a hot plate to prepare his meals in his closet, since he had no kitchen. "For months I ate rice and noodles in a closet," he recalled. Later he found a job as a waiter for $15 a day. He later described being a waiter as the hardest job in his life, but he kept it because he received a free meal with every shift. Ramos did not complete his studies at UCLA, but he later returned to school and earned a master's degree in international studies from the University of Miami.

CAREER HIGHLIGHTS

Starting Over in American TV

Almost a year to the day after arriving in the United States, Ramos began working for KMEX-Canal 34, a Spanish-language television station in Los Angeles. His initial salary of $28,000 felt like an enormous sum. As he gained experience, Ramos worked at refining his skills as a reporter. He polished his interviewing skills and toned down his heavy native accent so that he would be acceptable to the multicultural Spanish-speaking audience in the L.A. area. Ramos also strived to develop his own unique on-air style, adopting a natural, relaxed quality in front of the camera. This sense of ease, combined with his handsome face and piercing blue eyes, made him very popular with viewers.

—— " ——

"The morning program put me to the test in unimaginable ways," Ramos declared. "Even though that was not what I really wanted to be doing, it gave me the experience and confidence I needed to survive on a live television program."

—— " ——

Ramos covered a number of interesting stories in his first year on the job. He reported on the 1984 Olympics, held in Los Angeles. He also traveled back to Mexico to report on the terrible earthquake that struck the city in September of 1985. "Canal [channel] 34 was a wonderful school," recalled Ramos in *No Borders*. During his first year at Canal 34, Ramos also tried his hand at a new form of TV reporting: the live news program. Ramos later recalled his first efforts on the new live morning program, "Primera Edición" ("First Edition"), as a "disaster on air. We didn't know how to change cameras, and we were only able to read a few stories without making a mistake."

Yet for all the mistakes, Ramos's charm won out. The show became such a popular hit that it drew the attention of two executives from the Spanish International Network (SIN), the largest Spanish-language broadcaster in the world. They contacted Ramos and asked him if he would move to SIN offices in Miami, Florida, to host a morning variety and news program called "Mundo Latino" (Latin World). Ramos happily accepted, and in early 1986—just two years after arriving in the United States—he began his rise to the upper echelons of the television news industry.

Filing Reports around the World

Ramos further honed his television broadcasting abilities on "Mundo Latino," a program that was broadcast in a dozen countries around the world.

Ramos posing in 1994 with U.S. President Bill Clinton.

"The morning program put me to the test in unimaginable ways," he declared. "Even though that was not what I really wanted to be doing, it gave me the experience and confidence I needed to survive on a live television program."

Ramos's move to Miami also taught him a great deal about the politics of Spanish-language journalism in the United States. Within a short time of his arrival, he became acutely aware of the grim contest being waged between the city's Cuban-American and Mexican-American leaders for leadership of Miami's Hispanic community. That contest grew heated in the summer and fall of 1986 when a news personality linked to Mexico's PRI government nearly seized control of SIN's news division before being defeated. When that dispute was settled, Ramos—who had avoided taking sides in the struggle—was appointed co-anchor (along with Maria Elena Salinas) of "Noticiero SIN," the network's nightly news show. Suddenly, Ramos had become the face of the largest Spanish-language news source in the world.

As might be expected for someone so young, Ramos experienced some early bumps in the road as an anchor. "I was an erratic newsreader," he admitted. "I had a baby face and zero credibility." Despite his youth, however, he soon earned high marks for various reports on important issues facing Hispanics and Latinos in the Western hemisphere. He conducted interviews with important heads of state, ranging from the presidents of Guatemala and the Honduras to U.S. President George H.W. Bush (he has since interviewed every American president). Ramos also delivered first-hand reports from dangerous war zones around the world.

On several occasions these assignments placed Ramos in mortal danger. In 1989, for example, he and his crew were shot at by government soldiers while covering the civil war in El Salvador. Two years later, while reporting on the first Persian Gulf War in the Middle East, a military transport plane in which he was riding nearly crashed. Another life-threatening moment came in 2001, when he slipped into Afghanistan to cover the U.S. war against the Taliban, the fundamentalist Muslim government of Afghanistan that had been linked to the terrorist attacks against the United States on September 11, 2001. Ramos thought that he was traveling with guerrillas opposed to the Taliban, but one of the men revealed that he was a follower of terrorist mastermind Osama bin Laden. The guerrilla brought up his rifle to shoot Ramos, but the journalist escaped when he offered the rifleman a cash bribe.

_____ " _____

"I was an erratic newsreader," Ramos admitted about his early days on the air. "I had a baby face and zero credibility."

_____ " _____

A Famous Face

Today, Ramos and Salinas are regarded as fixtures on "Noticiero Univision" (which was renamed from "Noticiero SIN" after a change in ownership). During his tenure on the program, the show has expanded to 13 Latin American countries, and it is estimated that broadcasts of the news program now reach over one million viewers each night. In American cities with heavy Hispanic populations, the ratings for "Noticiero Univision" even surpass those of the nightly news programs for the major American networks, ABC, CBS, and NBC.

Like other famous American anchormen of the last 20 years—Dan Rather, Tom Brokaw, and Peter Jennings—Ramos also has become something of a celebrity in his own right. The research firm *Hispanic Trends* called him one of the "most influential Latinos" living in the United States in 2000; *Latino Leaders* magazine listed him as one of the "Ten Most Admired Latinos" in 2004; and *Time* named him as one of the 25 most influential Hispanics in America in 2005. He also has won numerous regional and national awards for news broadcasting, including Columbia University's Maria Moors Cabot Award in 2001.

During his long reign as anchorman of "Noticiero Univision," Ramos has also been a news story himself on a few occasions. In 1991, for example, his tough questioning of Cuban dictator Fidel Castro prompted Castro's bodyguards to roughly shove the journalist aside. A few years later, Ramos also posed tough questions to Venezuelan president Hugo Chavez, another Latin American leader who has suppressed press freedoms in his country. Perhaps his most memorable moment on television, however, occurred in December 2000. That month, Mexicans ended years of PRI rule and elected Vicente Fox as president. Ramos covered the story like a professional, but at one point the network cameras caught him breaking away to dance in the streets of Mexico City with other joyful countrymen.

Beyond the News

Though he has made his career on TV news, Ramos has frequently proclaimed that anyone who gets their news only from television is not well-informed. According to Ramos, many complex stories cannot be adequately explained in just a few minutes of television coverage. "I'm tired and sick of trying to explain the story in two minutes, of trying to give sense to a story about a war or a kid dying or an earthquake in two minutes," he has complained.

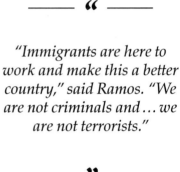

"Immigrants are here to work and make this a better country," said Ramos. "We are not criminals and ... we are not terrorists."

This frustration led Ramos to explore the written word as a way of conveying the complexities of the stories he covers. In 1997 he published *Detras de la mascara* (Behind the Mask), in which he described his impressions of people he has interviewed during his career. Two years later, he published *Lo que vi: experiences de un periodista alrededor del mundo* (What I Saw: Experiences of a Reporter Around the World). This memoir recounted Ramos's career in journalism, including some of his most exciting and frightening experiences.

In 2000 Ramos published *La Otra Cara de America*, which compared the immigration experiences of modern Latinos to the United States with those of earlier waves of U.S. immigration. Two years after its initial publication, this book became the first of Ramos's works to be translated into English, as *The Other Face of America: Chronicles of the Immigrants Shaping Our Future*. Since then he has explored immigration issues in two other books. In 2004 he published *Ola Latina* (*Latino Wave: How Hispanics Will*

123

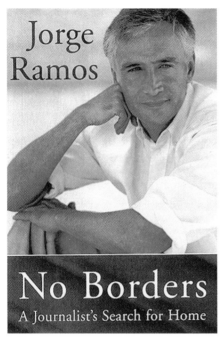

Ramos discussed his experiences as an immigrant in great detail in his autobiographical memoir, No Borders.

Elect the Next American President), which explores the growing political power of the Hispanic community in the United States. One year later he released *Morir en el Intento (Dying to Cross: The Worst Immigrant Tragedy in American History),* an account of a deadly incident in which 19 Mexican immigrants suffocated in the back of a truck being used to smuggle them across the U.S. border. In each of these books, Ramos focused on the complex social, psychological, and political issues that immigrants face as they try to build lives in the United States. These subjects resonated very strongly with Ramos, who is openly sentimental about his love for his home country, yet committed to the life he has built for himself in America.

Ramos discussed these warring emotions in great depth in 2002 in *Atravesando fronteras: un periodista en busca de su lugar en el mundo (No Borders: A Journalist's Search for Home),* his most popular book. This memoir traces his life from his early childhood through his years of spectacular career success. Upon its release, Ramos explained that he wrote it partly for his children. "I wanted to let them know who their father is and what I went through in the first 44 years of my life," he said. But he also wrote the book for English-speaking Americans who need to recognize "that immigrants are here to work and make this a better country and that we are not criminals and that we are not terrorists."

Ramos has also used other platforms to speak out on Hispanic issues in recent years. He writes a weekly newspaper column that appears in 40 papers in the United States and Latin America, and he is a frequent guest on U.S. television programs that discuss Hispanic issues. In 2002 he created a TV book club called "Despierta Leyendo" ("Wake Up Reading"), which appears monthly on Univision. The book recommendations he makes on this program have been credited with boosting numerous titles to the top of the Spanish-language bestseller lists.

Ramos's popularity and his willingness to speak out on political issues has led some observers to wonder whether he might some day run for political office, either in the United States or Mexico. He doesn't rule out the possibility. As of 2006, however, Ramos appears quite content to remain Hispanic TV's top newsman.

MARRIAGE AND FAMILY

Ramos has one daughter, Paola, from a late 1980s relationship with Gina Montaner, a Spanish television producer. Their relationship ended in 1989, when Montaner took Paola back to her native Spain. Though he described his separation from his daughter as "one of the most painful experiences" in his life, Ramos has continued to spend a lot of time with his daughter. In 1991 Ramos met his future wife, Lisa, and they were married on August 24, 1992. Their son, Nicolás was born in 1998.

Though Ramos calls Miami home, he travels constantly, and he admits that there "are long periods of time . . . when I am absent and distant." Despite the demands of writing and broadcasting stories from around the world, he treasures his time with his extended family. "Wherever Nicolás and Paola are, together, that is home," he wrote in *No Borders*.

HOBBIES AND OTHER INTERESTS

Many of Ramos's favorite hobbies involve sports. He plays soccer on the Univision company team. He also jogs to keep himself in shape, and in 1997 he ran in the New York City Marathon. Ramos also keeps his hand in a variety of other activities, from playing basketball with his daughter to solo ocean kayaking. Beyond his love of sports, Ramos commits himself to several hours of reading and writing every day.

SELECTED WRITINGS

Detras de la mascara (Behind the Mask), 1997
Lo que vi: experiences de un periodista alrededor del mundo (What I Saw: Experiences of a Reporter Around the World), 1999
La Otra Cara de America, published in English as *The Other Face of America: Chronicles of the Immigrants Shaping Our Future*, 2002
Atravesando fronteras: un periodista en busca de su lugar en el mundo, published in English as *No Borders: A Journalist's Search for Home*, 2002
Ola Latina, published in English as *Latino Wave: How Hispanics Will Elect the Next American President*, 2004

Morir en el Intento, published in English as *Dying to Cross: The Worst Immigrant Tragedy in American History*, 2005

HONORS AND AWARDS

Emmy Award: 1998 (2 awards), Outstanding Instant Coverage of a News Story; 2005, Spanish Emmy Award for "extraordinary contributions to Spanish-language television in the United States"
Maria Moors Cabot Award (Columbia University): 2001
Ruben Salazar Award (National Council of La Raza): 2002, for his positive portrayal of Latinos
Ron Brown Award (National Child Labor Committee): 2002, for "helping young people overcome prejudice and discrimination"
David Brinkley Award for Journalistic Excellence (Barry University): 2003
Journalist of the Year (Latin Business Club of America): 2004

FURTHER READING

Books

Contemporary Hispanic Biography, Vol. 2, 2002
Ramos, Jorge. *No Borders: A Journalist's Search for Home*, 2002
Who's Who in America, 2006

Periodicals

Current Biography Yearbook, 2004
Greensboro (NC) News & Record, Oct. 24, 2003, p.D1
Hispanic Magazine, Jan. 2001, p.62
Houston Chronicle, Oct. 16, 2002, p.1
Miami Herald, Oct. 8, 2000, p.M2
Publishers Weekly, Oct. 13, 2002; May 31, 2004, p.66
Television Week, May 30, 2005, p.26
Time, Aug. 22, 2005, p.53
Washington Post, Feb. 18, 2002, p.C2; Feb. 2, 2003, p.T10

Online Articles

http://www.hispaniconline.com/magazine/2001/jan_feb/CoverStory
(*Hispanic Magazine*, "Jorge Ramos: Making News,"
Jan.-Feb. 2001)

Online Databases

Biography Resource Center Online, 2006, article from *Contemporary Hispanic Biography*, 2002

ADDRESS

Jorge Ramos
Univision Television Network
9405 NW 41st Street
Miami, FL 33178

WORLD WIDE WEB SITES

http://www.jorgeramos.com
http://www.univision.net

Russell Simmons 1957-

American Entrepreneur and Business Leader
Co-Founder of Def Jam Records, CEO of Rush
Communications, Chairman of Hip-Hop Summit
Action Network, Creator and Producer of
"Def Comedy Jam" and "Def Poetry Jam"

BIRTH

Russell Wendell Simmons, known as "Rush," was born on
October 4, 1957, in Queens, one of the five boroughs in New
York City. His father, Daniel, was a teacher and administrator
for New York Public School District 29. His mother, Evelyn,
was a painter who also worked as the recreation director for
the New York City Department of Parks. Simmons's parents

both graduated from Howard University, where they met. A middle child, Simmons has two brothers: Danny is four years older and Joey (known as Run of the rap group Run-D.M.C.) is seven years younger.

YOUTH

Simmons grew up surrounded by artistic people. "There are no retiring people in the Simmons family—we are all creative, strong-willed, dynamic people." He describes his parents as highly educated, creative, and opinionated. During the 1960s, Simmons's father was politically active in civil rights issues and often participated in demonstrations, sometimes taking Russell along. His father also wrote poetry, some of which later appeared in Run-D.M.C. raps. Simmons remembers his mother as sophisticated, worldly, and very supportive of her sons' artistic interests. His older brother Danny was a painter, and younger brother Joey studied music and began writing his own songs at a young age. Meanwhile, Simmons was developing his own interest in music. "As a teen, my musical taste was forming, and it reflected my overall attitude toward life. I liked gutsy, cool music, nothing too pop. . . . The music I liked was very ghetto and gritty."

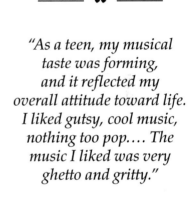

"As a teen, my musical taste was forming, and it reflected my overall attitude toward life. I liked gutsy, cool music, nothing too pop. . . . The music I liked was very ghetto and gritty."

Drugs and Gangs

In 1965 the Simmons family moved to Hollis, a working-class neighborhood in Queens. They lived in a small house on a neat suburban street of well-kept homes. But just a few blocks away was one of the busiest drug-dealing corners in Queens. When Simmons was a teenager, he got caught up in the drug world and began selling marijuana. He explained that his decision to sell drugs wasn't based on desperation or need, but rather on peer pressure and greed. "People were making money all around me," he said. "So from my silly teenage perspective, selling [made sense]. . . . It was a way to get the things I wanted—things that in retrospect were ridiculous and unnecessary."

Around this same time, Simmons was also involved with a gang called the Seven Immortals. "We didn't have guns and we didn't kill people as gangs do today. . . . We were really young and not that fearsome." They spent most of their time hanging out, not doing much more than riding the subway and trying to intimidate people. Things got a little rougher when some of the gang members began to vandalize stores and rob people. Simmons began to realize that there was no real purpose to being in a gang. He was finally convinced to leave it after another gang member was killed. "My gang career ended not long after the murder of a Seven Immortals member named Big Bear.... I guess it hit me that I already had a strong family, so why was I risking my safety like this?" Simmons left the gang, but continued to sell drugs.

———— " ————

"We didn't have guns and we didn't kill people as gangs do today," Simmons said. "My gang career ended not long after the murder of a Seven Immortals member named Big Bear.... I guess it hit me that I already had a strong family, so why was I risking my safety like this?"

———— " ————

A Close Call

Simmons has identified a pivotal moment of his youth in his autobiography *Life and Def*. In the book, he described a close call that made a big impact on him. While selling drugs, he was robbed by a neighborhood thief named Red. Simmons was pressured by the other drug dealers in the area, who expected him to do something about the theft. The next time he saw Red, Simmons and several others chased him and cornered him. "Somebody handed me a gun," he recalled. "It was the first (and only) time I've held a gun with the intention to shoot." When Red broke free and was running away, Simmons fired a shot and barely missed. "It's a feeling I've never forgotten.... In my heart I knew missing Red was the best thing I ever did." Simmons was 16 at the time.

Simmons does not glamorize this time in his life. He has made no apologies for his past, but he does regret that it might send the wrong message to young people. "I can't emphasize enough how reckless I was and how badly my life could have ended up," he stressed. "The sad thing is how many of my Hollis Crew peers were killed by the drug lifestyle. Some got hit in the head by thieves one time too many. Some got shot. Some died of AIDS in jail. The common denominator was drugs—they were killed pursuing a high or selling a high, by an addict or by their own addiction."

EDUCATION

Simmons's parents arranged for him to attend elementary school at P.S. 135, an integrated school in a white area of Queens, instead of P.S. 134, the neighborhood school in Hollis. For junior high he attended J.H. 109, a predominantly white school. Simmons cites these years as extremely important in forming his perspective on people, diversity, commonality, and the world in general. "Getting me into integrated schools was one of the best things my parents ever did for me, but not because the schooling was automatically superior. Even at that age I was an observer of people . . . a lifelong sociologist," he said. "I saw immediately there are no differences between whites and blacks in terms of what they want out of life. Everybody wants to be liked. . . . Being able to see beyond the obvious when it comes to black and white would be key not just to my career but to my life."

Simmons attended August Martin High School in Queens, graduating in 1975. During his senior year, his father got him a job at an Orange Julius in Greenwich Village. Although Simmons didn't like working there, he says, "Getting out of Hollis was good. It allowed me to see a wider world. The Village . . . would influence very much my vision of selling hip-hop later. It, along with SoHo, would be one of the places I would live in the future where I'd see not the differences in people, but the kinship among everyone. The attitudes that connected them is where the opportunity to sell to them existed." The job didn't last long, but it has been to this day the only regular, nine-to-five job Simmons has ever had.

"The first time I heard a rapper was in 1977. It was Kurtis Blow at the Charles Gallery on 125th Street. That changed my life," Simmons recalled. "I wanted to be in this business. Just like that I saw how I could turn my life in another, better way. . . . Just like that, I decided I no longer wanted to be involved in something like drug dealing that risked my life."

Discovering Rap

After high school, Simmons attended City College of New York in Harlem. He studied sociology and explored different parts of the city, meeting people who would shape the rest of his life. He was still selling drugs during this time, but that changed once he discovered rap music. "The first time I heard a rapper was in 1977. It was Kurtis Blow at the Charles Gallery on 125th Street. That changed my life," Simmons recalled. "I wanted to be in this business. Just like that I saw how I could turn my life in another, better way. . . . Just like that, I decided I no longer wanted to be involved in something like drug dealing that risked my life."

Simmons began following the progress of rappers who performed on street corners and in city parks, noticing the growing crowds that would gather to hear them. He met Rudy Toppin, who gave him the nickname Rush and started him in show promotion. To Simmons's surprise, he realized the toll that drug dealing had taken on his life. "Once out of that game, I felt better about myself and related to the world differently. I was more relaxed, happier, and not as edgy." Simmons eventually left college to begin promoting music shows full time.

CAREER HIGHLIGHTS

Starting Out

Simmons began promoting rap parties and concerts throughout Harlem and Queens with rapper Kurtis Blow (also known as Curtis Walker). The two had become close friends, and they worked together on show promotion. Simmons also represented Kurtis and other performers through Rush Artist Management, his newly formed company. He was committed to helping performers become successful, and he worked very hard to create opportunities for rappers.

In the early days, it was sometimes difficult to convince club owners to allow rappers to perform. At that time, disco was the most popular club music format, and most owners were reluctant to try something new. They didn't want to take a risk with rap, a relatively new style of music, because they didn't think club audiences would be interested. In order to put on a concert, Simmons would usually have to pay the night's costs up front, out of his own money. He counted on making the money back on ticket sales for the event. This strategy worked most of the time, and any profits were used to fund the next show.

One night no one came to the show, and so there were no profits. Simmons lost all of his money. He was completely broke, and went home looking for support. His father wouldn't help him because he wanted Simmons to go back to college and stop wasting his time on rap concerts. However, his mother had always believed that her sons should pursue their own goals. She gave him $2,000 from her personal savings. "It was that money that kept me afloat until Kurtis Blow broke and I entered the record business. That act of love and faith, which is what kept me in business at a key time, is my favorite memory of her."

The First Big Break

In 1979 Kurtis Blow's first single "Christmas Rappin'" became a hit. This was one of the first rap singles to receive widespread radio play. Although it was a Christmas song, it became so popular that radio stations continued to play it well into the summer. The song's popularity spread to other parts of the country and even crossed over to Europe. Simmons and Kurtis were invited to tour several European cities. This was a phenomenal first for a rap artist.

*Simmons's work with Run-D.M.C., shown here in 1988,
was one of his first big successes.*

"I remember when 'Christmas Rappin'' was a hit," Simmons reminisced. "I got a chance to get on a plane and go to Amsterdam, which, for me, was an amazing experience. I had never been on a plane at all. I went to Amsterdam in 1979 with Kurtis Blow and we were treated like—well, we thought we were kings. . . . These people watched us perform, and here we were in this big world with our own music." What impressed Simmons the most about that trip was being called "Mr. Simmons" by everyone he met on the tour. It was the first time anyone had ever addressed him that way. He recalled, "That was the best payment. It reminded me that I deserved it, that I was doing something worthwhile. I haven't gotten anything better than that since."

The success of "Christmas Rappin'" caused a stir in the rap world. Rush Artist Management, the company Simmons formed to manage and develop artists, was signing new talent every week. At that time, there were no other artist managers who were interested in rap. Simmons was busy producing records, booking shows, and helping artists develop both their music and their image. He was also traveling with Kurtis Blow, sometimes doing multiple shows in the same day. These shows brought the hip-hop sound to audiences that had never heard this type of music before.

It was an exciting time. Simmons and Kurtis were causing a revolution in the music world. At first, many people didn't know what to expect from Kurtis, who was often booked as an opening act for more famous funk or R&B performers. "We'd be up there setting up turntables on the stage and people in the crowd would mutter, 'We paid money to see a band.' But night after night people would be up dancing on their seats by the end of the set," Simmons recalled. "Davey D would just go out there and tear [it] up on the turntables, and then Kurtis would come on and rock the house."

―――― **"** ――――

"I remember when 'Christmas Rappin' was a hit," Simmons reminisced. "I got a chance to get on a plane and go to Amsterdam, which, for me, was an amazing experience. I had never been on a plane at all. I went to Amsterdam in 1979 with Kurtis Blow and we were treated like—well, we thought we were kings."

―――― **"** ――――

Creating Run-D.M.C.

During the same time that Simmons was managing Kurtis Blow, he was also working with his younger brother Joey to form Run-D.M.C., which would become one of the most important and influential acts in rap history. Joey had already gained a reputation as DJ Run, and Simmons paired him with Darryl McDaniel, better known as D.M.C. The trio was completed by Jam Master Jay, also known as Jay Mizell. Simmons created a total image for Run-D.M.C., dressing them in their trademark leather suits, hats, and sneakers, and encouraging them to stay true to their musical instincts. He also produced their records, calling the track "Sucker MCs" the "single most creative thing" he's ever done.

Run-D.M.C.'s self-titled first album was a hit before it was even released: five tracks had already been released as singles and had become very popular before the album as a whole was available. With Simmons's help, Run-D.M.C. had created a totally new sound. The unique sound of tracks like "It's Like That" and "Sucker MCs" was unlike anything being played on radio stations at that time. These tracks had no traditional musical elements

A still from the movie Tougher Than Leather. *Back row (left to right):
Jam Master Jay, Run, executive producer and director Rick Rubin,
executive producer Russell Simmons. Front row (left to right):
producer Vincent Giodano and Darryl DMC McDaniels.*

such as melody or bass line. The songs consisted mostly of driving drum beats, hand claps, LP scratches, and shouted rhymes.

Most record company executives and radio station programmers didn't know what to do with this new form of music. But Simmons knew that Run-D.M.C.'s sound was true to the street style of the people who gathered to hear rappers perform in city parks. He just needed to get the record into the hands of those people. The group signed a contract with Profile, an independent music label, to distribute the record. It quickly became the first gold rap album.

Once the tracks were finally being played on the radio, no one could believe how quickly Run-D.M.C. became popular. MTV began airing the video for "Rock Box," one of the tracks on this first album. This increased the group's exposure and resulted in many concert bookings and tours. Another historic milestone was reached when the song "My Adidas" became a hit. The group received a one million dollar sponsorship contract from Adidas, the first agreement of its kind between an athletic-wear company and a non-athlete.

In 1984, many of Simmons's performers were featured on the Fresh Fest tour. This tour included Run-D.M.C., Whodini, Kurtis Blow, the Fat Boys, and various breakdancers and DJs. Simmons described this as "the tour that put the boot to the ground for rap" and credited it with cementing Run-D.M.C.'s reputation as entertainers. During this tour, Simmons saw the power of bringing ghetto culture to audiences everywhere. "Run-D.M.C. didn't have to present a watered-down version of how they were or write a sellout hit to get MTV to change their programming. They simply had to be themselves, and fans responded."

Def Jam Records

Around the same time in 1984, Simmons met Rick Rubin, a white student at New York University who also wanted to promote rap music. Rubin had just formed a fledgling record label called Def Jam and was working to expand it. The two pooled their resources, and with $8,000 they founded Def Jam Records. The company operated out of Rubin's dorm room: Simmons managed the business and promoted artists, while Rubin scouted for new talent, produced records, and developed a broader musical approach for rappers. Rubin's knowledge of rock and punk helped rap artists like Run-D.M.C. develop a harder, edgier sound that incorporated elements of rock and punk styles.

Within two years, Def Jam had earned a reputation for supporting artists and allowing performers to express their individual style in unique ways. Simmons explains, "We had this vision that these artists were long term, that they had images that had to be protected.... We weren't going to change their music so it would sell more. We weren't going to sell them out or allow them to sell themselves out. We wanted to remind them to keep their integrity and promote that. We wanted to make sure that their images, their visual images, were out in the street, not just their music."

This strategy paid off. Def Jam grew to include many successful artists, including the 15-year-old L.L. Cool J and the first big white rap group, the Beastie Boys. Def Jam soon caught the attention of major record companies that were previously uninterested in rap. Columbia Records offered to promote, market, and distribute Def Jam's new recordings for a share of the profits. With financial backing and support from Columbia, 1986 was a landmark year for Def Jam. Albums like L.L. Cool J's *Bigger and Deffer* and the Beastie Boys' *License to Ill* sold many millions of copies. Run-D.M.C.'s *Raising Hell* produced rap's first top-five pop hit, a collaborative remake of Aerosmith's "Walk This Way." This track became the first rap video to get major airplay on MTV, and the collaboration with rock superstars Aerosmith introduced rap to an entirely new audience.

These successes continued to broaden the exposure and appeal of rap music. The Beastie Boys were instrumental in bringing rap music to suburban white audiences. L.L. Cool J's "I Need Love," considered to be the first rap love ballad, drew in more adult listeners as well as those with softer tastes in music. These releases were not calculated business decisions designed to increase record sales. On the contrary, Def Jam was simply supporting the rappers' individual artistic styles and growth.

The mid-1980s saw tremendous growth in the rap scene. Def Jam continued to sign contracts with new artists, including Public Enemy, Oran "Juice" Jones, and D.J. Jazzy Jeff and the Fresh Prince (who later developed a successful acting career as Will Smith). Simmons began exploring how the rap culture could expand into new media. He formed Def Pictures and produced *Krush Groove* (1985) in cooperation with Warner Brothers studios. *Krush Groove* was a rap musical based loosely on Simmons's own life. A somewhat surprising underground hit, the film grossed $20 million with its original release. He had less success with the 1988 film *Tougher Than Leather*, which critics called "'vile, vicious, despicable, stupid, sexist, racist, and horrendously made." Rick Rubin left Def Jam in 1988, and Simmons went on to develop more outlets for rap culture.

Defining Hip-Hop

The explosive growth of rap in the 1980s proved that there was a global market for the music. Rappers connected with audiences far beyond anyone's expectations. All different people from different backgrounds were identifying with rappers. There was a new culture emerging from what was at first simply a new form of music. This culture was known as hip-hop, and Simmons became one of its biggest promoters.

Hip-hop is often defined as modern, mainstream, young, urban American culture. It is primarily a music form but it also encompasses fashion, movies, television, advertising, dancing, language, and attitude. "When you are in a hip-hop environment, you know it; it has a feel that is tangible and cannot be mistaken for anything else," Simmons explained. "Hip-hop represents the greatest union of young people with the most diversity—all races and religions—that people have felt in America."

For the 1990s, Simmons adopted the goal "to present urban culture in its most true form to the people who love it, and to those who live it." He is widely credited with breaking down barriers between rap and mainstream pop music. "Black culture or urban culture is for all people who buy into it and not just for black people. Whether it's film or TV or records or advertising or clothing, I don't accept the box that [people] put me in."

Television and Movies

By 1990, Simmons had created Rush Communications to oversee Def Jam Records, Def Jam Pictures, and a new television production company. He had an idea for a weekly television comedy show that would feature African-American comedians. "Across the country, there [are] lots of discos and rap music clubs that become comedy clubs for one night out of the week. And those nights are always sold out. That told me there was an interest . . . and I jumped to service that market." "Def Comedy Jam" debuted in 1992 on the HBO cable television network. The show became so popular that for several years, it was the most-watched Friday night television program in the late-night time slot.

> "
>
> "When you are in a hip-hop environment, you know it; it has a feel that is tangible and cannot be mistaken for anything else," Simmons explained. "Hip-hop represents the greatest union of young people with the most diversity—all races and religions—that people have felt in America."
>
> "

Business continued to expand into different areas. In 1993, Simmons entered the publishing industry with *Oneworld* magazine. Also around this time, he sold the distribution rights for Def Jam recordings to Polygram for $33 million. The deal allowed him to retain complete control over Def Jam musical products, but freed more of his time to develop a growing list of new projects. His Phat Farm men's clothing line premiered in 1994, with the Baby Phat women's clothing line soon to follow. (In 2004, Simmons sold the Phat Farm/Baby Phat clothing lines for an estimated $140 million.)

Also in the 1990s, Simmons renewed his focus on television and movies. In 1995, he appeared in *The Show*, a film documenting the rise and popularity of hip-hop culture. He formed the Rush Media Company, a marketing and advertising agency that created an award-winning ad campaign for Coca-Cola in 1996. Def Pictures released several major movies, including *The Nutty Professor* (1996) starring Eddie Murphy and *Gridlock'd* (1997) starring Tupac Shakur. A syndicated television show called "Oneworld's Music Beat with Russell Simmons" began production in 1998.

Poetry and Politics

As the 1990s ended, Simmons's focus shifted once again. His attention was captured by spoken words, both for art's sake and to raise awareness of political issues. Starting from the belief that all significant change in the world is ultimately brought about by young people, Simmons found ways to give a new voice to the hip-hop community. "I feel this is our best generation, and our best opportunity to make a difference," he explained. "I plan to dedicate the rest of my life to doing what I can—through my businesses and other initiatives—to help empower people."

Simmons's "Def Poetry Jam" was a big hit on Broadway and later published in book form.

That empowerment process included giving young thinkers an outlet for their ideas in the form of "Def Poetry Jam." The first "Def Poetry Jam" was created as a television special for HBO. The show highlighted the re-emerging interest in poetry among young people and featured spoken-word performers along with poets. Simmons considered "Def Poetry Jam" a natural progression of Def Jam Records. "These young poets come out of the same spirit as hip-hop, but without music they're challenged to say something even more profound, something that stands on its own without a hot beat to back it up." The show developed into a series for HBO, a multi-city tour, and live theater performances on Broadway in New York City. "Def Poetry Jam" was widely acclaimed and won two prestigious awards, the 2002 Peabody Award and the 2003 Tony Award for Best Theatrical Event.

Another part of that empowerment process was political action. Simmons created the non-profit Hip-Hop Summit Action Network in 2001. The Network organizes Hip-Hop Summits, which are large meetings held in cities throughout the country. The Hip-Hop Summits get young people thinking, talking, and working on issues that are relevant to the hip-hop community. Past topics have included conflict resolution among hip-hop artists and accountability for hip-hop's political, social, and economic impact.

Defending Hip-Hop

In 2000, hip-hop surpassed country music as the third-largest music category in the U.S. By 2001, one out of every ten records sold in the U.S. was hip-hop. As the community of hip-hop fans grows, so does its number of critics. Hip-hop has attracted heavy criticism for what many describe as thug imagery and lyrics that glorify violence and mistreatment of women. As one of the most well-known promoters of hip-hop culture, Simmons is also one of its most determined defenders.

"Rap is an expression of the attitudes of the performers and their audience. I don't censor my artists. I let them speak," Simmons argued. This is important to Simmons because many hip-hop fans are growing up in the same environments that the artists portray in their lyrics and videos. "Almost all the records that people perceive as gangster records are about people frustrated, who don't perceive themselves as having any other opportunity and it's a description of their lifestyle more than it is an endorsement of it. And so that's something that, you know, people who listen closely to the music can tell. And people from the outside, all they can hear is the language. Well, real language is OK by me, and descriptions of real situations and a real reflection of our society, a part of our society, is important to me," Simmons explained. "My life has largely been about promoting the anger, style, aggression, and attitude of urban America to a worldwide audience. It is [the] contrast between street knowledge and traditional values that frightens mainstream people about hip-hop and other forms of street expression."

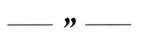

"My life has largely been about promoting the anger, style, aggression, and attitude of urban America to a worldwide audience. It is [the] contrast between street knowledge and traditional values that frightens mainstream people about hip-hop and other forms of street expression."

The Godfather of Hip-Hop

Simmons has been called the king of rap and the godfather of hip-hop. Sean "Diddy" Combs describes him as an inspiration, telling *Ebony* magazine that "If it weren't for Russell Simmons, I wouldn't be in the game. He gave the blueprint for hip-hop.... He knows how to break down color barriers without compromising who he is." Simmons credits much of his own success to his ability to connect with people regardless of background, race, or culture. "My audience is not limited by race. My core audience, my hip-hop audience, is black and white, Asian and Hispanic ... anyone who totally identifies with and lives in the culture.... That is the central philosophy that has driven my career."

Another important factor in Simmons's successful career has been his refusal to be limited in any way. "All of the businesses that I've gotten in, I got in because I didn't know I couldn't." He has cited real estate developer Donald Trump as his mentor, saying that Trump taught him a lot about achieving success in business. "Trump has been very influential in helping me expand my vision. Sometimes I talk to Donald two or three times a day."

Although Simmons maintains six business offices (three in New York City and three in Los Angeles), he does most of his work at home. He is never without his two cell phones, which ring constantly. His work day usually begins sometime in the afternoon and normally lasts well into the night. He visits an average of 15 different clubs a week, scouting for new talent and observing the hip-hop scene. He tries to stay as close to the hip-hop community as he can.

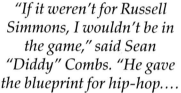

"If it weren't for Russell Simmons, I wouldn't be in the game," said Sean "Diddy" Combs. "He gave the blueprint for hip-hop.... He knows how to break down color barriers without compromising who he is."

Simmons's future plans are focused on his social and charitable projects. "I'm hopeful that I can be a better participant in relieving some of that suffering I have seen. I find that as you get older you just realize that there are more people in the universe than just yourself. I think we're all connected.... Tolerance is what it's all about."

MARRIAGE AND FAMILY

Simmons is married to former supermodel Kimora Lee. They met at a fashion show in which Kimora was modelling. They were married on the Caribbean island of St. Bart's in 1998. The wedding ceremony was performed by Simmons's brother Run (Joey), who is a minister. Rev. Run amended the wedding vows to have the couple promise to stay together "for richer, for richer." Simmons and Kimora have two daughters: Ming Lee, born in 2000, and Aoki Lee, born in 2002. The couple maintains an apartment in Greenwich Village, a house in Saddle River, New Jersey, and a house in the Hamptons on Long Island, New York.

HOBBIES AND OTHER INTERESTS

Simmons practices yoga and meditates every day. He says that studying the spiritual teachings of yoga have had a profound influence on the way he approaches his work: "For any business to be successful in the long run, it has

Simmons with his wife, Kimora Lee Simmons, and their two children, Aoki Lee and Ming Lee, 2004.

to be conscious of the fact that giving is, and will always be, the foundation of your success. All the religious teachings say the same thing . . . that you reap what you sow. Reading the yoga sutras caused these basic ideas to resonate within me. I use the science and the practice of yoga and the reading of various texts to remind me of these basic truths on a regular basis."

Simmons follows a vegan diet, meaning that he does not consume any foods containing meat or other animal products such as eggs or cheese, and is known as an animal welfare activist. He has partnered with non-profit organizations such as PETA (People for the Ethical Treatment of Animals) and the SPCA (Society for the Prevention of Cruelty to Animals) on various projects intended to raise awareness of animal welfare issues.

Simmons founded the Rush Philanthropic Arts foundation to support arts programs for young people throughout the U.S. The Foundation is run by his brother Danny and holds major fundraising events every year.

SELECTED WRITINGS

Life and Def, 2001 (with Nelson George)

HONORS AND AWARDS

Moet & Chandon Humanitarian Award (Moet & Chandon Champagne): 1998
Lifetime Achievement Award (*The Source*): 1999
Black Enterprise Company of the Year (*Black Enterprise* magazine): 2002, for Rush Communications
Peabody Award (University of Georgia): 2002, for "Russell Simmons's Def Poetry Jam"
Tony Award (American Theatre Wing): 2003, Best Theatrical Event, for "Russell Simmons's Def Poetry Jam"

FURTHER READING

Books

Business Leader Profiles for Students, Vol. 2, 2002
Contemporary Black Biography, Vol. 30, 2001
Contemporary Musicians, Vol. 7, 1992; Vol. 47, 2004
George, Nelson. *Hip Hop America*, 1998
Gueraseva, Stacy. *Def Jam, Inc.*, 2005
Ogg, Alex. *The Men Behind Def Jam*, 2002
Simmons, Russell, and Nelson George. *Life and Def*, 2001
Who's Who among African Americans, 2005
Who's Who in America, 2006

Periodicals

Billboard, Nov. 4, 1995, p.32
Black Enterprise, Dec. 1997, p.66; Dec. 1999, p.78
Black Issues Book Review, Sep. 2001, p.43
CosmoGirl!, Feb. 2005, p.84
Current Biography Yearbook, 1998
Ebony, Jan. 2001, p.116; July 2003, p.168
Essence, Sep. 2004, p.50
Fast Company, Nov. 2003, p.76
Fortune, May 17, 2004, p.41
Inc., April 1, 2004
Nation, Jan. 13, 2003, p.21
Newsweek, July 28, 2003, p.40
People, July 1, 2002, p.97
Rolling Stone, Nov. 15, 1990, p.106
Time, May 4, 1992, p.69

Online Articles

http://www.businessweek.com/bwdaily/dnflash/jan2004/
    nf20040113_4406_db074.htm
    (Business Week Online, "Tapping the Spirit of Success: Entrepreneur
    Russell Simmons Thanks Yoga's Philosophy for Giving Him the
    Principles to Operate His Ever-Growing Hip-Hop Empire," Jan. 13,
    2004)
http://www.inc.com/magazine/20040401/25simmons.html
    (Inc.com, "America's 25 Most Fascinating Entrepreneurs: Russell
    Simmons, Rush Communications," April 2004)
http://www.pbs.org/wgbh/theymadeamerica/whomade/
    simmons_hi.html
    (PBS, "Who Made America: Russell Simmons, Cross-Marketing
    Culture," undated)

Online Databases

Biography Resource Center, 2005, articles from *Business Leader Profiles for Students*, 2002, *Contemporary Black Biography*, 2001, *Contemporary Musicians*, 2004, *Who's Who among African Americans*, 2005

ADDRESS

Russell Simmons
Rush Philanthropic Arts Foundation
512 Seventh Avenue
43rd Floor
New York, NY 10018

WORLD WIDE WEB SITES

http://www.defjam.com
http://www.hsan.org
http://www.rushphilanthropic.org

Photo and Illustration Credits

Black Eyed Peas/Photos: Christian Lantry/copyright © 2003 Universal Music Group (p. 9); Scott Gries/Getty Images (p. 14); Albert Watson/copyright © 2003 Universal Music Group (p. 21). CD covers: ELEPHUNK and MONKEY BUSINESS copyright © 2003 Universal Music Group.

Neda DeMayo/Photos: Mark Muntean (front cover, p. 23); Frank Staub (pp. 25, 30); Andrea Maki (p. 29).

Green Day/Photos: Eva Mueller (p. 34); Ken Schles/Time Life Pictures/Getty Images (p. 36); NBC Universal Photo/Paul Drinkwater (p. 43); Marina Chavez (p. 47). CD covers: DOOKIE and AMERICAN IDIOT copyright © 1998-2006 Warner/Elektra/Atlantic Corporation.

Freddie Highmore/Photos: Warner Bros. Pictures (pp. 51, 54, 57); Miramax Films (p. 53).

Tim Howard/Photos: Matthew Peters/Manchester United/Getty Images (p. 60); Chris Trotman/Getty Images (p. 64); John Peters/Manchester United/ Getty Images (p. 66); Simon Bellis/Reuters/Landov (p. 68).

Rachel McAdams/Photos: copyright © 2005 Richard Cartwright/New Line Productions (pp. 71, 80); Michael Gibson/TM & copyright © 2004 by Paramount Pictures (p. 76). DVD cover: THE NOTEBOOK copyright © 2004 New Line Productions, Inc. Copyright © 2005 New Line Home Entertainment, Inc.

Rosa Parks/Photos: William Philpott/Getty Images (front cover, p. 85); Don Craven/Time Life Pictures/Getty Images (pp. 88, 93); AP Images (p. 90); William J. Clinton Presidential Library (p. 95); Mandel Ngan/AFP/Getty Images (p. 96); Staff Sgt. Earle B. Wilson, Jr./Photo courtesy of U.S. Army (p. 99).

Danica Patrick/Photos: Donald Miralle/Getty Images (p. 102); AP Images (p. 104); Frank Polich/Reuters/Landov (p. 108); Brent Smith/Reuters/Landov (p. 110). Front cover: Jonathan Ferrey/Getty Images.

Cumulative Names Index

This cumulative index includes the names of all individuals profiled in *Biography Today* since the debut of the series in 1992.

    For cumulative general, places of birth, and birthday indexes, please see biographytoday.com.

For cumulative general, places of birth, and birthday indexes, please see biographytoday.com.

Biography Today

General Series

Biography Today **General Series** includes a unique combination of current biographical profiles that teachers and librarians — and the readers themselves — tell us are most appealing. The **General Series** is available as a 3-issue subscription; hardcover annual cumulation; or subscription plus cumulation.

Within the **General Series**, your readers will find a variety of sketches about:

- Authors
- Musicians
- Political leaders
- Sports figures
- Movie actresses & actors
- Cartoonists
- Scientists
- Astronauts
- TV personalities
- and the movers & shakers in many other fields!

"*Biography Today* will be useful in elementary and middle school libraries and in public library children's collections where there is a need for biographies of current personalities. High schools serving reluctant readers may also want to consider a subscription."
— *Booklist,* American Library Association

"Highly recommended for the young adult audience. Readers will delight in the accessible, energetic, tell-all style; teachers, librarians, and parents will welcome the clever format [and] intelligent and informative text. It should prove especially useful in motivating 'reluctant' readers or literate nonreaders."
— *MultiCultural Review*

"Written in a friendly, almost chatty tone, the profiles offer quick, objective information. While coverage of current figures makes *Biography Today* a useful reference tool, an appealing format and wide scope make it a fun resource to browse." — *School Library Journal*

"The best source for current information at a level kids can understand."
— Kelly Bryant, School Librarian, Carlton, OR

"Easy for kids to read. We love it! Don't want to be without it."
— Lynn McWhirter, School Librarian, Rockford, IL

ONE-YEAR SUBSCRIPTION
- 3 softcover issues, 6" x 9"
- Published in January, April, and September
- 1-year subscription, list price $62.
  School and library price $60
- 150 pages per issue
- 10 profiles per issue
- Contact sources for additional information
- Cumulative Names Index

HARDBOUND ANNUAL CUMULATION
- Sturdy 6" x 9" hardbound volume
- Published in December
- List price $69. **School and library price $62 per volume**
- 450 pages per volume
- 30 profiles — includes all profiles found in softcover issues for that calendar year
- Cumulative General Index

SUBSCRIPTION AND CUMULATION COMBINATION
- $99 for 3 softcover issues plus the hardbound volume

For Cumulative General, Places of Birth, and Birthday Indexes, please see www.biographytoday.com.

Biography Today
Subject Series

For ages 9 and above

Expands and complements the General Series and targets specific subject areas . . .

Our readers asked for it! They wanted more biographies, and the *Biography Today* **Subject Series** is our response to that demand. Now your readers can choose their special areas of interest and go on to read about their favorites in those fields. The following specific volumes are included in the *Biography Today* **Subject Series:**

- **Authors**
- **Business Leaders**
- **Performing Artists**
- **Scientists & Inventors**
- **Sports**

FEATURES AND FORMAT

- Sturdy 6" x 9" hardbound volumes
- Individual volumes, list price $44 each. **School and library price $39 each**
- 200 pages per volume
- 10 profiles per volume — targets individuals within a specific subject area
- Contact sources for additional information
- Cumulative General Index

For Cumulative General, Places of Birth, and Birthday Indexes, please see www.biographytoday.com.

NOTE: There is *no duplication of entries* between the **General Series** of *Biography Today* and the **Subject Series.**

AUTHORS

"A useful tool for children's assignment needs." *— School Library Journal*

"The prose is workmanlike: report writers will find enough detail to begin sound investigations, and browsers are likely to find someone of interest." *— School Library Journal*

SCIENTISTS & INVENTORS

"The articles are readable, attractively laid out, and touch on important points that will suit assignment needs. Browsers will note the clear writing and interesting details." *— School Library Journal*

"The book is excellent for demonstrating that scientists are real people with widely diverse backgrounds and personal interests. The biographies are fascinating to read." *— The Science Teacher*

SPORTS

"This series should become a standard resource in libraries that serve intermediate students." *— School Library Journal*